Frank W. (Frank Welles) Calkins

Frontier Sketches

Frank W. (Frank Welles) Calkins

Frontier Sketches

ISBN/EAN: 9783337144180

Printed in Europe, USA, Canada, Australia, Japan
Cover: Foto ©ninafisch / pixelio.de

More available books at www.hansebooks.com

BY

FRANK W. CALKINS

CHICAGO:
DONOHUE, HENNEBERRY & CO.

CONTENTS.

		PAGE.
I.	A Piece of Frontier Strategy	5
II.	The Mystery of the $\underline{Y\,N}$ Brand	18
III.	Corson's Wife	28
IV.	The "Moaning Rock" at Bogey's Bend	40
V.	Mortimer Halleck's Adventure	54
VI.	The Mystery of the Valley	64
VII.	Followed	72
VIII.	Olaf Helgerson's Pay	83
IX.	A Wild Night-Ride	97
X.	Carlen and his Comet	105
XI.	Caught in a Blizzard	115
XII.	A Fortunate Cyclone	125

FRONTIER SKETCHES.

I.

A PIECE OF FRONTIER STRATEGY.

In the early days of the settlement of Wisconsin there were neither land surveys nor government laws by which lands could be held with perfect security by the settlers. There was, however, in most counties an unwritten law, much like that which governs claim-taking in mining districts, and which generally protected the claimant who complied with its requirements. These requirements which were adopted in nearly all the new communities as "neighborhood by-laws," and in most of them strictly enforced against all persons who tried to violate them, were usually something like the following:

The claimant, if he were of age or the head of a family, was entitled to one hundred and sixty acres of timber land and the same amount of prairie land, which he must first locate, and then proceed to measure by "stepping it off."

There was usually some one in every organized township who was regarded as an expert in measuring land. Eight hundred and eighty steps of three feet each along the four sides of a square, beginning at a given landmark and returning to it, were allowed as a quarter-section.

The corners were established on the prairie by marked

stakes, and in timber by blazing trees and carving the taker's name or initials upon them. Then within a reasonable time, say three months—the time was not definitely fixed—the squatter must build a cabin and move his family, if he had one, his effects if he had not, into it, and there make his home until the land should be surveyed and "come into market," when. by appearing either himself or in the person of the "township bidder," at the regular "land sale" for his district, bidding the minimum price, one dollar and a quarter an acre, and paying the money to the registrar of the land-office, he received a government patent which made his claim valid and final.

It was not well for an interloper to attempt to jump one of these claims, or to bid more than the minimum price above a claimant who had complied with the by-laws of his district.

Generally, as I have said, the squatter, who complied with these "right of discovery" land laws, was safe enough to hold his claim, and if he had not the ready money saved to pay for it at the land sale, he could easily borrow it of money-lenders in his district. But sometimes there were disputes, in which whole neighborhoods took sides, and occasionally a squatter's claim was the scene of an affray in which blood was shed.

Two young men, Jacob and Jared Stebbins, who lived in the region between Blue Mounds and the Wisconsin, very early in the history of that country, belonged to the pioneer class above mentioned. Their father had moved up there from Galena some time before the Black Hawk troubles, and, though they were but lads of sixteen and seventeen, they had taken part in the defense of Mound Fort, and in the battle of Wisconsin Heights.

As they grew up and Jake came of age, they became ambitious to have land of their own. They had helped clear grub, break up, fence and cultivate one hundred acres of land on their father's "patent" in Mound Creek Valley, and now it was high time to begin for themselves.

Up to this period the broad Wisconsin, unfordable except in the driest seasons, had acted as a check to the tide of Northern and Western settlement in their district. There was much choice land upon the other side, and some two years before Jake was twenty-one the boys had been across the river hunting, and had staked and blazed claims for themselves—two "quarters"—upon one of which they had subsequently erected a snug log cabin, which they had covered with boards of their own make.

They spent the greater part of two winters in this cabin, hunting and splitting rails during the short days, and during the spring, summer and autumn while working on their father's place, they watched jealously for any movement toward a settlement on the "other side."

The winter before Jake came of age several other claims were taken, above their own, on the west side of the river, on Sac Prairie, one of the most fertile prairies of the state. The boys now determined to move over finally so soon as they should gather the spring crops upon their father's place.

In March, upon going home from their claim, they left their cooking utensils and other belongings inside the cabin, and closed the door and window by nailing some heavy strips across them. It was not until May, after corn planting, that they moved across the river. They swam over two yoke of steers, their breaking team, and rafted across their wagon, ploughs and some other effects. It took them nearly all day to cross, and it was late in the evening when they reached their cabin.

The cabin had been built in the edge of the valley timber, and they had cleared a space around it. As they drove out into this open space, they were surprised by the yelping of a dog, which came rushing toward them, and flew at the faces of the steers, so that they halted and lowered their horns to fight off the brute. Jared ran forward and drove the animal away with his whip, giving it a cut which sent it back to the cabin.

"Somebody's here?" said he.

Jared went forward. The dog snarled at him from under the covered wagon as he approached. As he came up to the cabin, he saw that the boards had been ripped from the door, and that a light was shining through a crack.

"Hallo, thar!" he called, standing close to the door.

There was a moment of waiting, a murmur of voices inside; then the door swung inward, and the tall, gaunt figure of a middle-aged woman stood in the open space.

"Who be ye?" she inquired, gruffly.

"I'm one of the owners of this claim," said Jared, "an' wo'd like ter shar' the cabin with ye till we c'n get some supper."

"Wal' ye can't come in hyer!" said the woman, coolly. "This hyer claim an' this hyer cabin b'longs

"Who be ye?" she inquired, gruffly.—Page 8.

ter us?" and she stepped back to shut the door in his face.

Jared was hot-blooded and was naturally angry at this turn of events. He sprang towards the closing door, and threw all his weight against it. The woman was large and strong enough to have offered stout resistance, but she was taken by surprise; the door flew out of her grasp, back upon its hinges, and Jared was propelled against her with a force that made her stagger half-way across the room.

Jared had gained admission, but found himself facing two big, bony men, who had arisen from their stools before the fire-place as he burst the door in.

They sprang at him, knocked him over, sat on him—one on his shoulders and the other on his legs—and then, with buckskin straps, proceeded to bind him hand and foot.

Jared struggled for a moment, and then, finding it useless, gave it up. He was soon relieved of the weight of his captors, but lay helplessly bound upon the floor.

All this had happened so quickly that when Jake, who had heard the scuffle, had tied the steers and come cautiously up to the door, gun in hand, he found himself confronted by the muzzles of two rifles, which protruded through a crack which had been made by removing a board from the nearest window.

"Drop that gun!" came from within the cabin.

But instead of dropping his weapon, the quick-witted young settler sprang to one side, and ran behind the wagon, under which the belligerent dog was still barking. Then he called to his brother:

"Say, Jerd, have they hurt ye?"

Jared shouted back that they hadn't, but that two men had tied him hand and foot.

Jake picked up a club and threw it at the dog to drive it away; then he called to the men to know what they meant by such outrageous acts. One of them—the old man—answered back that they had taken up a man for assault and battery, and meant only to protect themselves and their rights.

Jake told them they had no business inside the cabin, which belonged to himself and his brother; that this claim had been made and held for two years, and that they were liable to prosecution for assault on his brother.

The elder man answered back that he and his son had found an old trapper living in the cabin; that they had bought his right to it, and laid claim to the land, and, what was more, they should hold it against all comers. It was also stated that a colony of settlers from Illinois had come in some three weeks before, having crossed the river at "The Portage," and squatted along on that side; that a general meeting had already been held, and the usual regulations adopted, and that the speaker inside the cabin had been chosen constable until a regular election was held.

The young fellow was astounded and chagrined at this intelligence. The situation was puzzling enough, for he saw that these claim-jumpers had greatly the advantage over him. He and Jared could really prove nothing; not a settler on the other side whom they knew had ever visited them here or knew of the location of their claim except by heresay. Their only callers had been two or three stray trappers and an occasional Winnebago Indian who had at various times spent a night with them.

It was one of those trappers, a rascally-looking fellow whom he remembered he had disliked, who had pretended to sell this claim to the present occupants—and there was a whole neighborhood to stand by them in possession.

The situation was discouraging even if Jared had not—according to the code of the region—been lawfully arrested for an assault. Jake went out near his own wagon and sat down on a stump to think.

The night was not dark; the moon was shining faintly and a light wind was moving the tree tops, and as Jake sat with his face between his hands in a brown study, the figure of a person came across his range of vision. A boy emerged from the woods a short distance west of the cabin and came toward him. As he approached the dog ran out and began leaping upon him.

"Hullo, mister! w'at ye doin' out hyer?" The voice was that of a lad of fourteen or fifteen.

Jake answered, warily, that "he'd jes' druv up a bit ago, an' was wonderin' whore thar might be some water fer the oxen." He added that he thought it rather late to wake people up to find out—there was no light that could be seen from the cabin.

"Oh, I'll show ye," said the boy. "It's 'bout forty rod, though, the way ye'll hev ter drive t' git down ter the crick."

"That don't make any differ'nce—the distance," said Jake. "I want to camp by water,"—which was true enough, as matters had turned out.

Thereupon he untied his oxen, turned his wagon

about and drove after the boy, who led him back very nearly over the way he had come. Jake, looking back as they entered the timber-line, saw the cabin door swing open, and some one come out and look after them. But fortunately the boy was straight ahead and could not be seen, and the man, who had probably come out to see what was going on upon hearing the wagon rattle, turned again and entered the cabin.

It was fifteen minutes' drive down to the creek, by the nearest approach for a wagon, but, as Jake well knew, the stream could be approached on the opposite side of the cabin, which was situated in a bend of it, by a very short cut through thick brush. It was from that quarter, in fact, that he and Jared had brought their water for cooking purposes.

However, it just suited a plan which had flashed upon him that the boy should be at the pains of selecting for him the best camping-place—it got them out of sight and hearing of the cabin.

Jake walked well up by the steers and talked to the boy as they went forward and learned, as he had expected, that the lad was the son of the man who had jumped his claim. The boy said he had gone over to a neighbor's who had just moved into a new log-house one mile west and was to have stayed all night, but finding that a number of land-seekers had claimed the neighbor's hospitality, he had spent the evening at play with their boys and returned. He said his father's name was Burrel.

They reached the creek, and Jake, having quickly matured a plan of action, stopped his oxen and while untying a long, slender lead-rope from the horns of the "near" steer at the head of the team, kept the boy near his side by talking to him.

When he had secured the rope, however, he turned, flung an arm around his listener, and with a quick trip threw him to the ground. The boy struggled and screamed with fear and anger, but Jake quieted him with a stern command and then, holding him fast, told him just what had happened at the cabin, and also gave him a truthful account of his own and his brother's labor in making the claim, which had been jumped regardless of their rights.

"An' now, youngster, I'm goin' ter tie ye up, an' bring yer ole dad ter terms, an' the more ye cut up the wuss it'll be for ye."

The boy evidently believed his story and saw both the point and the justice of the case, for he sullenly submitted, gritting out between his teeth that "Dad 'n' Bob 'll get ev'n with ye fur this."

Jake tied his prisoner securely, unhitched his oxen and turned them loose, with the yokes on, to graze, and then, getting some quilts out of the wagon, made a bed under it, picked up the captive and laid him upon it. He then ate a cold bite of bread and meat, and taking his rifle went slowly back to the cabin.

When he arrived there he again seated himself upon a stump and gave his mind to thought. He had gained one advantage, at least, he could exchange prisoners and get his brother free, which had been his object in so roughly treating the boy, but could he do anything more?

He determined to try. Accordingly he got up and stole softly behind the covered wagon where he had stood before—the dog seemed to have exhausted its animosity or else it had followed the wagon and gone rabbit-hunting.

Jake now shouted loudly at the cabin

"Ho, Burrel! Burrel, I say!"

There was a movement inside, a light shone through a crack and an angry voice—the old man's again —replied: "Wall, what ye yawpin' 'bout now?"

Jake briefly related the story of the boy's capture, only being interrupted every few seconds by ejaculations of wrath and chagrin from his auditors, or at least from two of them. Jared was listening also, and Jake heard him give a shout and a hearty laugh of triumph at the conclusion.

For a moment there was confusion inside the cabin, and a gabble of excited discussion, then the door opened cautiously, and Jake heard somebody—evidently a woman—crying piteously.

"Oh, they'll kill 'im! they'll kill my babby!" she moaned.

"Shet up!" said one of the men, roughly.

"Say, mister!" he called, poking his head out of a crack in the doorway.

"Now, look hyer!" called Jake, sharply, "none o' that! Keep inside ef ye want to keep a whole skin."

The head was hastily withdrawn.

"Now, lookee hyer!" repeated Jake, "I'm a-goin' ter hold this hyer cabin in a state o' seige till ye come ter my terms. My terms is these:

"Yer turn my brother loose; give 'im ev'ry gun ye've got an' let 'im bring 'em out hyer to me. Then yer pick up yer duds, 'n' bring 'em out 'n' pack 'em in this wagon 'n' take yerselves off 'n this claim, n' when ye've done that I'll turn yer boy loose, 'n' when ye've gone 'n' took a claim 't ye've got a right ter squat on, 'n' git settled onto it, yer c'n send one o' yer neighbors after them guns. Now yer c'n jes' do that er I'll hol' ye in thar till the crack o' doom, 'n' yer boy 't's tied up out thar in the woods c'n stay thar till the b'ars eat 'im up, er the wolves, 'n' they's plenty o' both round hyer. I've got plenty ter eat in my pockets 'n' good shelter commandin' the winders 'n' door."

At the close of this speech there was another wail inside the cabin. The woman, rough as she was, loved her boy and was terribly frightened, and the men seemed subdued and impressed with the gravity of the situation. After a long parley the men, moved by the entreaties of the woman and greatly to Jake's surprise, did accept them and sent Jared out with the guns.

They brought out their household goods and the men sullenly packed them in the wagon while Jake and Jared with the guns stood guard at a safe distance. They got up their oxen and hitched them to the wagon, and then the woman, who had silently helped bring out their bedding, clothing and cooking utensils, broke down again, and begged that the boy might be "turned loose 'n' fetched."

This was more than Jake could stand, and though he knew the lad was safe and fairly comfortable, he had tied him so that he felt certain he could not get loose. He, therefore, left Jared with two guns to guard the claim-jumpers and went and got the boy. The whole party then drove off without a word.

It was nearly two weeks before a neighbor with whom they had become acquainted, and who sided with them upon learning all the facts in the case, came over and got the guns, and brought the information that the Burrels had settled about twelve miles down the river. He had previously told them that he and some other neighbors, who had elected the elder Burrel a constable, had not been acquainted with the family long, having only fallen in with them while "moving."

After getting acquainted with all the new-comers of their neighborhood the two boys found good friends and good neighbors among them.

II.

THE MYSTERY OF THE Y N BRAND.

Six or eight years ago horse and cattle thieves were exceedingly troublesome to the stockmen of Montana and northern Wyoming. During a year's stay in those regions I heard many accounts of daring and successful robberies, of narrow escapes on the part of these raiders, and of various curious expedients employed by them to accomplish their object, which was, of course, to drive off stock which did not belong to them.

One of the most bold and yet cunning attempts at cattle-stealing, perhaps, ever made, occurred about that time on the South Cheyenne range near the Wyoming and Dakota lines. I do not know that the story was ever told outside the region in which it happened: but, whether or no, it seems worth telling now.

It was just at the close of the Indian troubles about the "Hills," when cattle men had newly discovered the many advantages of the range of country lying immediately south and west of the Black Hills. It would, in fact, have been impossible to have carried out so daring a scheme on an older and more closely guarded range.

One of the first ranches to occupy a portion of this excellent grass region was built at Dead Cedar Forks on West Dry Wood, and was owned by the Cheyenne Cattle Company. It started with two thousand head of stock, and its brand duly recorded in the nearest stock journals was *J V*, the initials of an old ranch man and chief stockholder, Joe Villemont. The letters were simply formed, about eight inches in height and eight inches apart, and were stamped upon the broad sides, always on the right of the company's cattle, and in smaller letters upon the left hips of its horses.

"Old Joe," as Villemont's men called him, had always been averse to the cruelty of the big, complicated brands which disfigure the cattle upon so many ranges, and which must cause so much suffering in the stamping, and afterward until the wound heals. Accordingly he had always used the simplest and smallest brand that would identify his stock.

At about the time the J V ranch, as it was called, was established, several other cattle-owners came into the region, bringing large droves of cattle, and built ranches on Horse Head and Hat Creeks, and at the head of White River, and the Running Water, and the "L Z's," "Circle Bars" ⊖ "K—23's," "Goose Eggs," "000" and others, took their places with the "J V's" upon the range.

The circuit of a "round-up" was soon determined upon, and the cow-boys of each ranch soon made themselves familiar with the various brands upon their riding circuit.

It was at the third general round-up, in June of the second year, that the boys working to the northwest discovered a new brand upon that part of the range, and searching their record-book of Nebraska, Wyoming and Dakota brands could find no marking to correspond. The new brand was "bar Y N" thus, $\underline{Y\,N}$ stamped upon the right broad side, and supplemented by a new moon upon the right hip.

It was a camp on Lightning creek, a number of the

"Circle Bars" and "J V" men, who first found stock carrying the "bar Y N" brand, as they named it. They found several steers and eighteen or twenty cows bearing it, in the first bunch they rounded up and corralled at the Lightning Creek branding pens. The markings seemed rather fresh, and the calves which were running with the cows were not yet branded.

There was no little speculation in the camp that evening, after the stock-book had been inspected by the foreman, as to where these cattle belonged. It was supposed that they must be strays from some recently established ranch farther north—one probably that had just run in a lot of fresh-branded stock and had not yet advertised its brand.

As the camp moved north and made a new branding pen on Old Woman Creek the bar Y N stock became more numerous until it was calculated there must be a hundred and fifty or more of them; and the out-riding cowboys began to keep their eyes open for signs of a ranch.

The mystery seemed to be solved one evening by the appearance in camp just at supper time of a horseman who reined up with a hearty "How do?" and alighted. He was a slim, dark-looking fellow, dressed in a well-worn suit of corduroy, and wearing the regulation slouch hat and high top boots.

"Well," said he, as the foreman of the camp came forward, "Well, I suppose you've discovered a new brand on your range down here,—the 'bar YN,' eh?"

The foreman said they had, and then asked if he represented that stock, to which the stranger replied that he was superintendent of the ranch to which it belonged, a ranch which had been newly established on the Little Missouri range, that they had shipped out a lot of Minnesota cattle in March, and driven them down from the Northern Pacific, having hay enough on hand to keep them from running down until grass should start up fresh in April.

They had expected to hold them without trouble, but there came a three days' blizzard, which the J V and Circle Bar men had experienced also, from the north, caught a lot of them out, and ran them off to the south. There were about seven hundred of these new cattle gone from their ranch, he said, and they had found them scattered all the way from Belle Fourche to Hat Creek.

He then drew a Montana stock journal from his breast pocket and pointed out his brand advertised as the property of the "Minnesota & Montana Cattle Company," and went on to say that he had brought down three of his men to begin at the southernmost point at which their stock was to be found, and work back toward home, gathering the cattle as they went:

"We'll take what calves you leave us," he said, laughingly, "for you will be through with your branding before we fairly get to work!"

He remarked that his camp, temporary, of course, was on a creek about twenty miles east, and that he had merely stumbled upon the round-up by chance while looking for his own brand.

His story, perfectly plausible and established by an advertisement in an accredited stock journal, made him heartily welcome at the cow-camp, where he was immediately invited to take supper, and, as it rained that evening, he shared the foreman's bed, under the cover of a big supply wagon.

It was about a week after this that the round-up broke camp, and in the meantime two other cow-men were met in search of bar Y N stock. Rather rough-looking fellows they were—hardly up to the standard of "number one punchers" the men thought them. Two of the J V boys, "Griff" Mosher and Tom Dodd, with an extra pony and a week's supplies, were left to look up several ponies which had strayed from the camp at Indian Creek, while the others moved to another part of the range.

Griff and Tom "rustled" around lively for a few days, picked up all of the ponies but two, five had strayed, and giving those up for lost had started from Lightning Creek to go to the J V ranch on Dry Wood. They were riding down into the deep valley of a small run in search of water and a camp for the first evening, when they came upon a large bunch of cattle grazing upon the bottom and side hill.

Upon approaching they discovered the brand bar Y N upon the nearest ones, and struck by the size of the drove, rode through them to discover, if possible, whether they all had that mark. It seemed so; at least, they could see no other markings except the new moon looking remarkably fresh upon the right hip of each creature inspected.

"Hum," said Griff, as they rode forward, "them fellows hev rounded up a big lot of strays right here, haint they now? Say, Tom, don't it 'pear sort o' strange that they haint a spotted critter in the whole bunch?"

Tom cast his eyes over the lot with some astonishment.

"That's so," he admitted; "not a one."

"And say," said Griff, pulling up with sudden energy, "if that big yellow steer there with the wide horns haint the one we hed such a tussle with a-rebrandin' him over at Old Woman last fall, I'll eat my hat."

Tom emphatically coincided with him.

"Yes, an' what's more," fairly shouted Griff, "I can see a dozen cows I'd swear to as J V's this minute! Here, cut loose the horses an' let's down that red heifer thar with a fresh brand on 'er, an' hev a look at it!"

It was the work of three or four minutes for these practiced "ropers" to catch the heifer, throw her, and examine her brand. It also took but a hasty scrutiny to discover that an old marking of J V had been changed to Y N by adding fresh "lean tos" to the original letters, with a bar and the new moon to make the deception more complete.

Griff and Tom wasted no time, but set their wits at work, to plan a capture of the daring rascals, or, at least, to take steps at once to prevent them from running off the stock, as—from the gathering of so large a bunch—it was evident they intended doing soon.

Luckily, as they believed, the fellows had not discovered their presence in the valley, and were probably camped at no great distance above or below. As there were known to be four of them at least, the boys felt that it would be too risky to attempt to cope with them alone, and they determined to ride to the ranch at Dead Cedar Forks, and rally a crowd if any men could be found there.

They mounted, passed through a narrow draw to the creek and up another to the high ground beyond, and then rode hard all night, changing ponies frequently, and only stopping twice for water, and a half-hour's rest at noon or a little before they reached the J V ranch.

There was no one there except Lame Johnnie, the cook, and he had not seen a man, he said, for five days; didn't know where any of the boys were or when they'd be in.

Johnnie himself could not ride on account of his wretched legs; and while they were off hunting up a crowd the thieves might drive the cattle through to Montana and sell them.

Not an hour was wasted; the two bold fellows determined to make an attempt to recapture the stock unassisted. Arming themselves with Winchesters from the ranch in addition to their six-shooters, and selecting four of the best ponies from the corral, they rode swiftly back over the route they had traveled in the morning.

They gave themselves three hours' sleep that night, and the next morning halted at the creek where they had found the bunch of stock with the stolen brand upon them.

As they had feared, the cattle were gone; there was not a creature except a few head of L Z and Circle Bar stock to be seen in the region. But after two hours' search to the northward of where they had struck the stream, they came upon a well-defined and fresh trail of a lot of cattle going north, and knew they were upon the right track. The cattle had been started the day before, as near as the boys could judge, or the day after they had seen them.

They followed the trail at a racking gait until it became too dark to trace it without difficulty, then picketed their tired ponies, ate a cold lunch, and gave themselves up to a night of refreshing and much needed sleep.

All the next day they rode hard upon the trail, but did not come up with the thieves, who, they concluded, were pushing the stock at a terrible rate, probably fearing that they were pursued, as, indeed, for aught Griff and Tom knew, they themselves might have been within plain sight of some or all of the thieves, while making the discovery of the fradulent brand.

It was easy to keep hidden among these breaks and gulches.

It was not until late in the afternoon of the third day's chase that they sighted the drove just descending into a narrow and cañon-like valley of a tributary of the Belle Fourche.

Believing the thieves would stick to this narrow valley in order to keep well hidden, the boys circled, rode rapidly around them, and descended into the valley in their front, as they could tell by the cloud of dust that rose continually above the herd. They reached the level of the stream at the mouth of a gulch about sundown.

Knowing that the cattle thieves would be on the alert, the two cowboys had formed no plan save that of immediate attack upon them from the nearest point of vantage and the most unexpected to the attacked that could be gained.

The spot they had happened upon was well adapted to an ambush. They picketed their ponies some rods from the mouth of the gulch and out of sight, and then the determined fellows, with their Winchesters and revolvers, and abundance of ammunition, placed themselves behind a small bank and awaited the approach of the robbers as they urged the stock along the cañon.

The cloud of dust rolled down, and the leaders of the herd came in sight climbing out of a gulch a few rods distant. Yells and the cracking of stock whips could now be heard above the trampling and lowing of the cattle.

It was growing dusk, and the thick dust which rose from the dry, grassless soil of the cañon made it impossible to see more than a few rods with certainty. But soon at the tail of the herd two horsemen appeared, then another, then a fourth. They were riding not far apart, the nearest about fifty yards away, and rather dimly outlined in the dust and growing darkness.

Griff and Tom laid down their Winchesters, and with self-cocking revolvers opened fire upon the miscreants.

The first shots had no other effect than to cause the thieves to leap from their saddles and get behind their ponies. That they did not immediately ride out of range was no doubt owing to the fear that they had been surrounded, and that these shots were merely to drive them upon the muzzles of other guns upon the other side or in the rear.

They were not altogether cowards, either, for they returned fire at once, and for a few moments the cañon witnessed one of those fierce shooting affrays which sometimes occur between the outraged citizen and the desperado of the plains and mountains.

"Crack! crack! crack!" the thieves fired across their horses' backs at the heads and shoulders which Griff and Tom offered as marks, while the incensed and excited cowboys emptied their revolvers, and then caught up their Winchesters and "pumped" forty-five's in rapid succession.

These last weapons settled the affair speedily, their length and steadiness gave a better and truer aim than could be got with revolvers.

First a pony went down, then one of the thieves got a bullet in his leg and led his horse away while he limped at his side. The man whose horse was shot took to his heels and ran away. One of the others exposed himself while mounting, and rode away hanging across his horse's wethers. The other sprang upon his pony, and galloped off up the cañon.

In three minutes from the time the firing began the thieves were whipped, "cleaned out" in Western parlance, and gone, and the two plucky cowboys had come off without a scratch.

They dared not attempt to follow up their advantage, however, but rode immediately after the stock, which they succeeded in getting out of the cañon, and twenty miles on the route toward home before morning.

After that they took it leisurely, only keeping a sharp lookout, and taking turns in guarding the stock closely at night. They saw no more of the thieves who had, no doubt, had enough of cattle stealing for once.

The Cheyenne Cattle Company rewarded this bold exploit as it deserved, by raising the wages of Griff and Tom each from forty-five to sixty dollars per month.

III.

CORSON'S WIFE.

It would be hard to find in the Rocky Mountains a rougher stage road than that which runs between the mining hamlets of Thunder Gulch and Squaw Forks. Indeed, if a worse road could be found, there are few persons who would care for a seat in the coach of the most careful driver.

This road is twelve or thirteen miles long. A few years ago a lady who ventured to ride over it called it "The Twelve-Mile Horror," and by this name the road is known to miners and travelers of the region. That the name is deserved the writer can testify, for he knows it to be truly a rambling thread over dizzy precipices and among black, gaping cañons.

There are places along the verge of cliffs and around the jutting points of yawning gulches where the coach seems literally suspended in mid-air, and the rider, glancing out over the wheels into the sheer, gaping space below, hastily pulls down the "flaps," closes his eyes, and leans dizzily back in his seat, not daring to look a second time.

For five years Gideon Fletcher, or "Gid," as he is commonly called, has driven the stage once each day, Sundays excepted, from Squaw Forks to Thunder Gulch and back. Of course, he has occasionally missed a trip, when slides or heavy falls of snow along the line have prevented him from running. Yet during all his fifteen hundred "round trips" he has never met with an accident serious enough to cause the loss of life or limb to his passengers.

So trusty and sure-handed a driver is he that the "contractors of the line" will have no other, and they pay him double wages to keep him upon this particular stretch of their route. Only once has a coach been demolished or a horse killed under his management; but on that occasion he met with a double accident, under circumstances so stirring and heroic as to be well worthy of narration.

It was some two years after Gideon had begun driving the coach upon this road that one day, as he came out from eating his dinner at "The Rough-and-Tumble House" of Thunder Gulch, a pale-faced young woman appeared at the rude gate, and beckoned to him.

"Are you the stage-driver that drives the stage to Squaw Forks this afternoon?" she asked, as he came up.

"I reckon I'm the chap yer lookin' fer, mum," said Gideon. "Want ter go down? Start in half a hour."

The woman glanced about nervously, as though fearful of being overheard, and then she said, hurriedly and in a low voice:

"I'm from Corson's Camp. I'm Corson's wife; but he—they all—abuse me dreadfully, and the baby too. Look here," and she threw an old bonnet she wore back from her forehead, and showed a great fresh scar across one temple.

"I got that last night. They do it when they're drunk, and they're drunk most of the time. Night before last one of 'em threatened to throw my baby into a hot spring. He said he'd 'kill the little imp, he would,' and oh, I can't, I don't dare to stay there any longer! I'm the only woman up at the camp, and

"I'm from Corson's Camp. I'm Corson's wife."—Page 29.

to-day the men are all up at Big Horn Spring prospectin' for a new place, and so I've come to you to see if you won't take me away from this dreadful place.

"I've no money with me, an' no friends nearer than Denver. My folks live there, and I would have wrote to 'em to come and take me away if I dared; but I knew if Corson got wind of it before they got here he'd kill me and the baby, too; for though he's my husband he's the most horrid and wicked man I ever saw, except the gang he keeps around him. Oh, *will* you let me go with you?"

"Wal, now, I sh'd smile!" answered Fletcher, in his hearty way. "You jest go 'n' git yer baby 'n' yer fixin's, 'n' we'll git out o' these diggin's in a jiffy."

"Oh, I daresn't come here to start," she replied; "but in an hour I'll be down at the mouth of the 'Gap' below. If I should come here, Corson would find out soon as he comes back that I'd started off with you, and they'd like enough catch us before we'd got down to the Forks.

"Some of 'em may be back any minute; like enough they're there now; but I'm going to sneak away with baby somehow, if they are. There don't seem to be anybody hangin' round here now. All off but the women folks, I s'pose, and it looks like I'd have a good chance to get off without anybody's knowin' how or where I went," and with this she turned and sped away.

"I'll wait for ye, sure," Gideon assured her as she started.

He hung about the stable of the Rough-and-Tumble longer than usual that noon, pretending to one of the women that came out presently that he had to "fix" something about his harness before he started on the return trip.

"Everybody's gone off crazy 'bout the new *placer* up at Big Horn," they had told him at the table, "'n lef' nobody but ther women folks 't the Gulch."

In about an hour from the time he had finished dinner, Gideon and his coach were in waiting at the mouth of Melcher's Gap. It was about half an hour later when the woman, with her child in arms, came hurrying breathlessly down to him. She looked behind her frequently, and he saw as she approached that her face was white with fear and suspense.

The baby, a wretched little year-old object, dressed, like its mother, in mere rags, turned its poor and pitiful little face upon the driver with a wan smile that, as he said, "fetched" him "clear to the boots."

"Oh, you *must* drive fast," cried the poor woman, as she clambered into the coach without waiting for the proffered help, "for they've come back, as I was afraid! Corson and two of the men, and they're going to break camp and move up to Big Horn this afternoon. They daresn't trust me there alone, for I *am some* good to 'em in cookin' and keepin' camp. I knew this was the last chance to git free, so I took the baby and started down to the spring for a pail of water, and when I got out of sight I just run for here, and you must go, go, for they'll sure be after us!"

"I'll *go* fast enough," answered Gideon cheerily, "an' don't you be afraid they'll ketch us neither on them leetle mountain ponies."

But though he spoke with such assurance and determination, he did not feel at all sure of the outcome of a race if the men at Corson's camp should soon discover the woman's flight and follow. He felt that he had taken an extremely hazardous exploit, considering the dangerous route he had to drive over and the characters of the men, who, he had not a doubt, would be upon his trail within the next half hour.

The spring at Corson's Camp he knew was in a ravine at the head of Melcher's Gap, and as this cañon was the only outlet in that direction, Corson could not long remain ignorant of his wife's line of flight after he had discovered, as he soon must, that she was truly gone.

But the woman and her baby, in such evident and distressing need of rescue, had "fetched him," and the brave driver, looking to his revolvers to see that the chambers were all loaded, drew in the lines and urged forward his horses at as great a rate of speed as the nature of the road would warrant.

For a half hour or more the coach rattled forward at a dangerous pace, for these first few miles were the roughest part of the road. Up and down it went through deep gorges, scaling precipitous "hog backs," and swaying far above the verge of cavernous cañons. From the point of every turn that commanded a view of the trail behind, Gid cast anxious glances backward, to note if anyone were yet in pursuit.

At the "half-mile stone," which was supposed to mark a spot midway between Thunder Gulch and Squaw Forks, was a height from which a good portion of the road for two miles back could be seen, and here it was that the driver discovered, indeed, that Corson and his men were following them. A single glance sufficed to reveal them—three horsemen—riding at a breakneck gallop over the crest of a long hog-back some mile and a half in the rear of the coach.

"A flight for life," thought Gideon, and he cracked his long whip above the ears of the already fretted stage-team. The horses were not unwilling to go faster, however, on the contrary they seemed nervous and frightened at such unusual driving, and sprang forward at a pace which the driver soon found it necessary to check by vigorous pulling at their reins.

"Are they coming? Did you see them?" screamed the woman, frightened at the swaying and rocking of the stage as they rounded a curve.

"Oh, *we're* all right!" the driver shouted back, evading a direct answer. "The road ain't bad, hyar! An' I'm a-tryin' ter make up fer whar *'tis.*"

The coach tore along, pitching crazily down into deep gullies, and swaying wildly above the crests of abrupt cliffs or the sides of gulf-like ravines.

It was quite a number of minutes before Gideon caught sight of the pursuing horsemen again, but when he did, as they came around the point of a mountain spur, they had gained perceptibly upon the coach, and the question of being overtaken had narrowed to one merely of time. And now the driver began to canvass the chances of making a successful defense when he should be finally overtaken.

There was a point nearly two miles ahead, where, if he could only reach it, the road ran along the foot of a narrow ledge and above a precipitous gulch, and, where he thought he might halt the coach behind a sheltering point of rocks, and "stand off" their pursuers with his revolvers. He was now determined at every hazard to keep the woman and her child out of the clutches of her pursuers.

With this goal and end in view, then, he drove with a recklessness, which in any less urgent case would have been mad, indeed. More than once the poor woman screamed with fright, as the hack lunged forward or careened over, and ran several yards on two wheels.

But Fletcher kept a steady and strong rein on his animals, and threw his weight to one side or the other as the coach rocked and threatened to overturn.

Several minutes passed in this mad flight, when, glancing back at a smooth turn, the driver caught another view of Corson and his men; they were now pressing hard upon him. There was but a few minutes more to spare in racing, but Gideon had reached a point where, if no accident should occur, he felt certain of gaining the narrow pass.

His horses were sweating profusely from fright and exertion, but still seemed full of energy.

On, on, they flew. It was wonderful that the coach kept right side up, while the poor frightened woman inside clung frantically to her seat with one arm, and to her babe with the other.

Another half-mile was passed safely, and Gideon felt a thrill of triumph as he struck the mountain spur, upon the other side of which he felt sure of making a successful stand against their pursuers. Both at the Gulch and the Forks, he was known as a "crack shot" with his revolvers, and those three fellows, he thought, with no little judgment, wouldn't care "to run up agin 'em," when once he had gained the shelter of the jutting rocks on the other side.

But just as he reached the point of the spur, and when too late, he remembered a dangerous curve in front, where, going at their present rate of speed, the hack must inevitably be thrown off the ledge by its own momentum. It was a short turn upon a steep bench with a ledge above and a chasm below.

He threw all his weight in a backward pull upon the lines, but the team, now thoroughly frightened and wildly excited by their furious run, refused to obey the reins, and plunged recklessly ahead.

They were now within a few rods of the fatal turn, and Gideon, foreseeing instant catastrophe, dropped the lines, sprang over the back of his seat, and catching both woman and child in his arms, jumped out with them upon the upper side of the road.

They were scarcely out of the hack when the vehicle "sloughed" off the road, overturned, and, as it did so, wrenched the team off the narrow "dug-way."

The poor animals scrambled resistingly for an instant, then one lost its footing and fell; the other plunged over it, and coach and all went crashing into the bottom of the gulch below. Gideon had time to note this, as he says, even while trembling with his precious freight from the bank of the spur, against which he had leaped, into the road-bed.

Luckily the bank at that point was of earth instead of rocks—the ledge was but a few steps further on—and the three, though shocked and jarred, were unharmed by their violent exit from the hack.

Gideon, however, did not stop an instant to note whether the woman or her child were injured, but gathering the baby on one arm and grasping its mother's arm with his free hand, ran forward, carrying the one and fairly dragging the other.

Just a few steps beyond the ledge were several big boulders on the lower side of the road. To gain the shelter of those before Corson and his men came in sight was now Gid's object.

Before the boulders were reached, he could hear the clatter of hoofs around the curve. The men were in close pursuit and riding hard, but by dint of great exertion Gideon reached the rocks with his charges a minute or two before the pursuers rounded the point.

"Set close behind hyar," he commanded the woman, "and hyar, take your babby 'n' keep es quiet 'n' es cool es ye ken."

Then he drew a revolver from one of the holsters at his hips, and dropping upon his knees at a spot where he could peer through between two of the boulders, cocked the weapon, and leveled it upon the road preparatory to halting the fellows with a shot as soon as they came in sight.

He had not a second to wait before the leader appeared at a point just beyond where the stage and team had gone off the bench and over the cliff.

It was Corson himself, but he had "slowed up," and before Gideon could make up his mind to fire, he suddenly drew rein, and gave utterance as he did so to a loud and excited oath.

He had discovered what had happened to the stage by means—as was afterwards proved—of a sheep-skin seat cushion, which had been flung out of the back as it overturned, and had lodged on top of the ledge.

The other two men came up almost instantly and halted, and then the three dismounted and talked excitedly together—though Gideon could not distinguish what they said—and one of them went forward and peered long and intently over the ledge.

But either he dared not go near enough to the verge of the precipice to see plainly to the base, or he could not clearly make out the wreck on account of the chaparral thicket below, for, after gazing a minute, he shook his head decidedly, as though convinced that passengers and all had gone over, and then all three quickly remounted, wheeled their ponies about upon the "dug-way," and disappeared as rapidly as they had come.

"Unyhugh!" grunted Gideon, with great satisfaction, "ye think ye've ran us over thar 'n' smashed the hull outfit, don't ye, 'n' ye've skipped mighty sudden for fear 't' sumun 'd come along 'n' diskiver yer deviltry, haint ye?"

Then he told Mrs. Corson to get up, and taking the child from her arms—the scared little thing had slept as quiet as a young partridge in hiding—helped her to rise and led her out upon the road.

The woman had seemed like one dazed while lying there in hiding, but now that she understood that the man she so feared had really gone she plucked up courage, and declared that she could easily walk the remainder of the way to Squaw Forks—there being no habitations at that time between the two points.

They reached the little town after a wearisome tramp over the rough road.

Their arrival and the story of their adventure and escape created great excitement among the miners, who gathered at one of the stores that evening, and raised two hundred dollars to give to the woman, besides paying her stage fare in advance to the nearest railway station where she could take a train for Denver.

The coach and the team were discovered the next day, a shapeless wreck, having taken a clear plunge of nearly one hundred feet. Only the mail was rescued.

Corson and his gang " pulled up stakes" and left the region immediately, and it was well for them that they did, for as the story of the woman's sufferings became known, the irate miners would surely have lynched them if they had not taken themselves away.

IV.

THE "MOANING ROCK" AT BOGEY'S BEND.

A daily newspaper widely read in the West devotes a page of each Saturday's edition, seven columns or so, to collections of ghostly doings, as related by local narrators in various parts of its own and surrounding States. These tales and brief accounts are entirely devoted to modern and, if many of them are to be believed, "well-authenticated" ghosts, surprising as this may seem to the reader who has not the advantage of an acquaintance with the "spook" columns of the journal in question.

There are stories, indeed, of haunted houses in southwestern towns where even the electric light has failed to "lay" their nightly and mysterious visitants. This local revival in ghostly matters and beliefs gives good proof of the strength and persistence of inherited tendencies.

In the backwoods annals of forty or fifty years since we expect to find strong traces of superstition, tales of weird and supernatural happenings. It was the writer's good fortune lately to listen to one of these old-time accounts in a story of a haunted rock, the incidents of which were told him by one who took part in the adventure, and are well remembered by old inhabitants about Bogey's Bend.

Bogey's Bend of the Wisconsin river received its name from its earliest settler, a Canadian Frenchman, who had married an Irish wife in his native province, but after a time moved westward with a numerous family and finally settled upon a fine tract of land in a sweeping bend of the Wisconsin, the only land fit for cultivating, in fact, of several square miles contained within the curve, the remainder being swampy, heavily timbered, and subject to over-flow. Hence it was a lonesome spot, and other settlers had been content with the fertile valleys and plateaus of the bluffs which skirt the river valley. A spur of those bluffs projects across the valley at the lower end of Bogey's Bend, terminating in a razor-like ridge, sharply descending and abruptly ending at the river's bank. Numerous big rocks, jagged, and broken, crown the "hog-back" of this ridge, and at the very extremity, protecting this bluff, indeed, from the wear of a swift current, stands a pinnacled rock projecting about seventy-five feet above the ridge and nearly twice that distance from the water's edge.

To the right of this rugged sentinel, calling the river its front, a densely-timbered swamp stretches for several miles, while immediately at its left the earth of the bluff has caved off, leaving an extremely high and steep bank plainly bearing the marks of an old landslide. And it was told by the old trappers of the region and also by an aged Winnebago chief, known as an occasional visitor throughout the surrounding settlements, that the caving off of this huge bank some thirty years before had buried a party of adventurers who, with a Winnebago guide, had drawn their canoes in there and camped for the night upon the river shore beneath the beetling bluff.

Ever since that time, so the trappers and the Indian maintained, the spirits of these unfortunates had hovered about the big rock—had made it their home, in fact; and almost any night of the year they might be heard moaning and sighing in a way that made the listeners shiver. When the wind blew strongly up river on a wet night, our old trapper claimed, it was "jes beas'ly terrible ter hear thar carryin's on." And the old Winnebago said:

"Heap spirit make um noise, scare Injun a heap."

The trappers and hunters, who in this locality, as in all others throughout the Northwest, had preceded the settlers, giving a nomenclature which has generally stuck to prominent landmarks and streams, had not failed in the matter of this mysterious rock, and its name, "The Moaning Rock," still clings. The stories which they told of the supernatural noises and sights which were to be heard and seen—for some of them claimed also to have seen strange things about the rock—naturally found a credulous reception among the more ignorant of the settlers, and in fact for several years the locality of the Moaning Rock was pretty generally avoided. Even among those who "poohed" at the idea of there being any ghosts at all, and boasted of having been to the rock and that nothing of the kind was to be heard or seen, very few, if any, had ever been known to go there in the night.

Some there were, of course, practical men, busied with work and improvement upon their new farms, who very sensibly paid no attention to any tales of the sort that infested this rock, and who had no interest in visiting the isolated spot.

Peter Bogey was one of these. He laughed when his children or wife repeated with awe the accounts they had heard of the "Moaning Rock," and would say good-humoredly:

"Fools dey ees ticker es de guss'oppers."

But to his Irish wife and the young Bogeys the rock was a veritable bugbear. The boys could scarce be got to go in its direction in search of the cows when the animals strayed that way. However, as "Al" Bogey, the oldest boy, got well along in his teens and began to extend his hunting excursions further into the swamps, he grew—like his father—skeptical of the ghosts and witches in which his mother firmly believed, and at length became so bold in one of his hunts as to track a deer directly up to the foot of the ledge above the crown of which towered the redoubtable rock. He had seen it once before from a height of bluff some half a mile distant—a safe point of view—beyond which few visitors ventured.

What he saw now was a steeple-like rock, triangular in shape, with rough, jagged edges and sharp projections, and growing beside it in a sheltering fashion a huge whiteoak-tree, some of the largest limbs of which had been turned aside in their growth by its nearness. Al could not but feel that it was a bold thing to stand there surveying the rock, and felt not a little uneasy, notwithstanding his lately-aroused skepticism. He lingered for some time, and though he felt strongly the influence of the old tales he had listened to, and the weird lonesomeness of the spot, he neither saw nor heard anything of an alarming nature. Yet he knew that night was the real time to settle the matter—at night, when the wind "blew strong up river." And as he wandered towards home, having lost the trail of the deer upon the hard dry soil of the ridge, he came to the determination to find out for certain whether the story of strange noises and sights at the "Moaning

Rock" were true or not. He knew a young fellow, Jet Ferris, over on Bear Creek, whom he was sure he could get to go with him.

Jet was a great hunter, afraid of nothing, and would as gladly be out all night as all day if there were any fun or excitement to be had.

He said nothing at home of his visit to the rock or of his plan, not wishing to arouse the fears and opposition of his mother, who believed in real ghosts and wizards, and that only evil could befall those who tried to pry into their affairs.

It was September, and Al had not long to wait for a wet, drizzly day which freed him from work and also promised the right sort of a night for his adventure, the wind blowing "up river," or nearly so. As soon as his morning chores were done he took down his father's rifle and set out for the home of Jet, on Bear Creek, four miles distant. Upon reaching young Ferris's home he was told that "Jet hed went up t' the Birch Bluffs t' shoot pa'tridges," and was asked to come in, "set by the fire an' dry yer clo's."

But he declined the invitation, saying:

"Wet clothes ain't nothin'."

And, well knowing that the game Jet was hunting would be found that day upon the sheltered side of the bluffs, he set out after the hunter again, and, after a two hours' tramp, succeeded in finding him.

Jet, after his fashion, gave Al a boisterous greeting, and then readily agreed to his proposal to spend the night, or a part of it, at the Moaning Rock.

"I ben awantin' ter dew it," said Jet, "fer a long time, but I didn't know of nobody as I thought 'd wanter go long 'th me 'n' I couldn't scrouge myself clean up ter the p'int of goin' alone; but along of you I ain't afeared."

They spent a large part of the day in hunting, returning to Jet's home with back-loads of pheasants and squirrels. Then, after an early supper, or rather, a late dinner, they started for the Moaning Rock—a trip of four miles or more along the tops of the Bear Creek Bluffs.

It was yet broad daylight when they reached the rock. They went boldly up to it, walking along the base and gazing up at the ragged sides and pinnacled tops.

"No spooks up thar es I c'n see," laughed Jet. And then, as it still lacked some time of growing dark, he proposed that they should go down into the swamp with the dog and "see 'f he can't stir out a coon er a wild cat."

To this plan Al eagerly agreed. Having a lantern with them to light their way home they set it down at the base of the big oak to await their return.

After a half hour's unsuccessful beating about in the nearer parts of the big timber swamp it began to grow dusk, and they turned back for their night's vigil. The wind, instead of "going down with the sun," had risen considerably, and was blowing stiffly among the tree-tops as they emerged upon the river bank at the foot of the big rock. There was a fine rain falling also, and they started at once to pass around the base of the rock and climb the ridge to the shelter of the big oak which branched out partially on the leeward side of its neighbor. They had not ascended one-third of the way when a strange, weird sound broke out above their heads—a long-drawn wail that wound up in almost a shriek.

Al Bogey, who is now a man considerably past middle age, says though he fought three years in the war he can remember no moment of his life of such terrible fright and suspense as the one in which he first listened to this wail from the Moaning Rock. He cowered down to the very ground, expecting instantly some awful vision to present itself. But Jet stood boldly up and listened intently while yet another mournful wail broke forth and quavered, at first low and plaintively, then increased to a shrill whistle, then died away only to be followed by others, sounding sometimes singly, sometimes a number in unison.

"Nothin' in the worl' but the wind up 'mong them snags 'n' jags of rock," he said presently, and in a triumphant, conclusive tone that brought Al to his feet with a heart that soon began to beat naturally with the sudden conviction that Jet was right. He, too, now that his "right mind" had returned, could recognize the old familiar whistle of the wind, as it had sounded from his baby days around the chimneys and the roofs of the log houses in which he had lived.

He was breathing easy again when suddenly an entirely different and more appalling sound jarred upon his ears, and once more sent a chill creeping over him.

C-r-r-a-a-i-k-k!

It was a harsh, discordant scream, such as might have issued from the mouth of the ugliest wizard of all his mother's category.

"Mercy, Jet! he exclaimed; "what's that?"

"Huh!" grunted the stolid fellow, "a feller that

runs in the woods oughter know that sound; it's two o' them big boughs up thar that's growed crosswise a grittin' agin each other. I've hearn 'em do that a hundred times in the woods. Now them sounds," he went on, "is jest the long 'n' short o' the hull o' this here sperrit business; an' es fer seein' things, why eny body es is too skeered ter know them sounds could see a 'most any thing they 'magined, I sh'd jedge."

This made Al feel rather small, but he owned his cowardly feeling.

"I was skeered, Jet, that's a fact, 'n' if I'd ben alone," he said, "thet rock would 'a' ben howlin' with sperrits."

"O, wal," replied Jet, with intent to comfort, "you haint traipsed the woods es many years es I have, else ye'd know'd them sounds. Thar she goes agin'—"

S-c-r-r-e-a-k!

"Now let's go up," he concluded, "an git our lantern 'n' strike fer home."

The wind whistled and screamed overhead as they climbed, and when they reached the trunk of the old oak a new wonder greeted them—the lantern was gone!

Although fast growing dark it was still light enough to have discovered the lantern had it been near the spot where they had left it; it was a bright new one, and its polished tin base could almost have been seen in utter darkness. In vain they lit matches, and finally built a fire from dry sticks gathered within shelter of the rock; their luminary was gone, and no trace of it could be found. The wind could not reach the spot where it had sat, and the dog had been at their heels coming up from the hunt; therefore something or somebody unknown to them had taken it away.

"Wall," said Jet, scratching his puzzled head, "this here comes the neardest to speritool perceedin's of anything I've hearn on 'bout this rock."

It was about this time that the dog began to show signs of excitement. Suddenly putting his nose to the ground he ran out to the river bank along the top of the land-slide and began barking furiously.

The boys piled more sticks on the fire and then followed the animal.

"That's whar our lantern's gone, " declared Jet. "Don't know what's got it, but that dawg's follered it fur's he could, sure. Thar's somethin' round here that ain't no sperrit, fer that dawg don't foller nothin' that don't make tracks ner leave no smell."

They cautiously approached the edge of the bank where the animal was jumping about in noisy excitement, and peered over into a black depth which the oncoming night had made murky and forbidding enough.

Nothing was to be seen or heard; the wind's roar drowned even the swash of the current which ran below.

"Thar's somethin' down thar somewhar," declared Jet, positively.

"Shucks!" said Al. "How could anythin' be down thar on the sides of that slide?"

Just then, as if in answer to the question, there flashed out below a little to their left a thin stream of light. It came from the bank and projected in a funnel-shaped glare, like the light from a bull's eye lantern.

They were startled, and yet the streak of light shone out into the blackness with such a natural, cheerful gleam that there could be no doubt of a genuine flame behind it, queer as the situation seemed.

"What'd I tell ye?" exclaimed Jet, triumphantly. "Some feller down there with our lantern."

"Fishin' mebbe," suggested Al. "Must be farther down than it looks."

"No," said Jet, "it's comin' right out o 'the centre o' the bank not more'n forty feet below. Somebody's in a cave or a hole down thar, 'n' if 'tw'a'nt fer this howlin' wind I sh'd expect 'em ter hear the racket up here 'n' be pokin' ther heads out."

The dog had suddenly left them again, and a moment later they heard him barking directly below and nearly beneath them.

'Thar—see!" exclaimed Jet. "Thar's a path goes down; it's out here by the rock." And he ran to the fire, and, gathering the unburnt ends of several flaming brands, in his hands, arranged a torch.

"Now, come on," he said; "let's find the path."

"Ain't you feared?" asked Al.

"Shucks, no," replied the plucky fellow; "it's only some ol' trapper that's got a good thing long of these banks which nobody won't come near, 'n' the cute ol feller's dug a hole down thar so's ter keep hid up."

This theory re-assured Al, and, hiding their guns under a dry ledge, they passed around the rock to the edge of the bank. After a moment's careful search the path was found leading from between two boulders obliquely along the steep incline. By the light of Jet's flaming sticks they could trace the narrow roadway several yards in advance. It had plainly been cut into the bank by the aid of tools, but it proved a ticklish affair, barely sufficient for safe passage in daylight, and after descending carefully the slippery way for a dozen steps or so, Jet halted.

"'Taint safe," he announced to Al, who was cautiously following, while he held the torch above his head. "'Taint safe to go no furder, slippery 'n' narrer, 'n' what's more, the rain's goin' to put this light out d'rectly."

All this time the dog had barked energetically ahead, but as Jet finished there came the booming reports of a gun, followed by a sharp canine yelp either of fright or pain. It was evident almost instantly that the animal was more frightened than hurt, for, peering ahead under his waning light, Jet saw the dog bounding up the path. Instinctively the torch-bearer threw himself back against the bank, and the dog sprang past, brushing him smartly, but not pushing him off his feet. Al was not so lucky; the brute, both frightened and hurt, as it afterwards proved, struck him squarely upon the legs, knocking his feet from under him.

Instantly the luckless lad was sent sliding down the slippery incline at a rate of speed which took his breath and left him no time for thought or action. Luckily he started feet first, and instinct, of course, made him clutch the earth of the bank with either hand, thus keeping his body in the same position; at least he supposes so, for he had sense enough to feel that he struck the water feet first, and, after a strangling splash, was surprised to find himself standing up to his neck in the current and up to his knees in mud. It was the season of low water, and the stronger portion of the current turned further out by the rock above had allowed the water to fall away from the bank and intervening bed to fill partially with the earth washed down from above.

As soon as he got his breath Al began the struggle to free his feet, which it took some time to do, as the velocity of his "slide" had driven his legs into the sticky material with no little force. He succeeded at length, and then setting to work as best he could in such a depth of water and such darkness, got off his boots and most of his clothes and made a bundle of them. He was a good swimmer, and as the water was not very cold he struck boldly out into the current and swam down stream, using one hand and his legs, while with the other hand he clung to his clothes.

He had swum but a few minutes when he heard Jet's voice hallooing at him from the bank above. He gave an answering shout, to which Jet replied with a joyful whoop.

"Down a leetle furder here, Al," he shouted; "here's a good place ter climb the bank. And Al having rounded the bluff came in shore by the aid of Jet's light and was soon standing dripping upon the bank, while Jet, holding a dimly-burning brand, danced around him in a furor of delight.

"Hurray!" he said, "I thought ye was a goner. Mighty lucky there wasn't no stones ner stumps ter hit agin. Now git on yer clo'es, fer we must be gettin' out o' this. I brung down the guns, hopin' ye'd turn up all right, fer 'twont be safe fer us ter poke round up thar any more. They's a den o' thieves, er wuss, up thar in that bank."

After a weary, stumbling tramp over the bluffs, they succeeded in reaching Ferris's house in the valley. The family got up to listen to their story, and the dog was called in and carefully examined. Two slight buckshot wounds in the jaw and shoulder attested the truth of the boys' narrative.

By noon the next day nearly all the men and boys of Bear Creek had assembled, each armed with some sort of weapon, at the Moaning Rock.

But the inhabitants of the bank had flown; their den, a roomy excavation with a small entrance just large enough to crawl through handily, was found empty, and the hay or grass which they had used for beds had been scattered over the floor of the cavern and burned, thus leaving no scrap of anything by which their business or their number might be guessed. There were two paths, one leading to the ridge above, and the other to the water below, thus giving two avenues of escape, as they had, no doubt, a boat in hiding upon the river.

The bank proved not to be so steep as it appeared in looking from the top or bottom. The cave-dwellers, whoever they were, were evidently aware of the superstition investing the Moaning Rock, and had taken advantage of the protection it offered in seeking a base for some secret and, no doubt, illegal traffic.

The settlers at once concluded that they were counterfeiters, and probably they were right in so thinking, for the country at that time was exceedingly pestered with well-counterfeited bills of the State, or "Wild-cat" banks, as they came to be called later.

As the rain had obliterated all traces of flight, however, no attempt was made to follow this band, for it was evident from the size of the cave and the work that had been done that there must have been a number of them. That they had thought themselves discovered and were prepared for fight, even before Jet and Al had returned from the swamp, seemed evident from the taking of the lantern and their warning shot at the dog.

The cave remained a neighborhood curiosity for some years, and was inhabited for a time by wolves, but at length the wash of heavy rains wore away and destroyed all trace of both path and cavern.

The episode above related, however, broke the spell which had so long hung around the Moaning Rock, and Jet and Al got, as they deserved, no little credit for their plucky adventure.

V.

MORTIMER HALLECK'S ADVENTURE.

Among the many adventurous incidents of our frontier life in northwest Iowa, fifteen years ago, I recall one that befell a boy neighbor, Mortimer Halleck, in which his recklessness came very near causing his death.

There were five of us boys, who formed a little company of tried friends and pledged comrades. We hunted, trapped, boated, went skating and swimming together, and, when the first frame school-house was built, we occupied the two back seats, on the boys' side.

In our hunts after deer, wolves, badgers, and feathered game, we found an exhilaration such as I never again expect to experience in the tamer pursuits of life. We even felt an exultant joy in the fierce buffeting of the winter blizzards which annually descended upon us from the plateaus of Dakota.

During the regular season of bird migration, the resounding *golunk, golunk,* of the wild goose, the shrill *klil-la-la* of the swift and wary brant, the affectionate *qu-a-a-rr-k, quack* of the Mallard drake and his mate, with the strange, inimitable cry of the whooping crane, combined to form a sylvan orchestra, the music of which thrilled us with more pleasurable sensations than were ever awakened by the household organ or the town brass band of later years.

In the early spring, during the alternate slush, mud and freeze of the first thaws, there always occurred a short vacation from school and work, in which we gathered a harvest of fun, fur and feathers.

At this season, the low, flat valleys of the Little Sioux and the Ocheyedan rivers were covered six or eight feet deep by the annual overflow; and torrents of yellow snow-water, the melting of tremendous drifts, rushed down creeks and ravines.

As soon as these impetuous currents had gathered force enough to upheave the thick layers of ice in the river-beds and break over the banks, out came beaver, musk-rat and mink, driven from house and hole to take refuge upon the masses of ice and drift stuff which lodged in the thickets of tall willows that grew along the beds of these streams. Here they were obliged to stay until the water subsided, and here they often fell a prey to the rifle or shot-gun of the hunter.

We owned three boats in common; and as the men of the settlement were not particularly busy during the freshet season, we could easily persuade or hire them to load our skiffs on their wagons, and haul us eight or ten miles up the Sioux or Ocheyedan, for half a day's run down home, in which scarcely the stroke of an oar was necessary, after getting out into the main channel. Floating leisurely down, we were able to hunt muskrat, geese and ducks, which were plentiful on the water or on the banks.

Beaver were scarce, but we occasionally got one. A mink or two, a couple of dozen musk-rats, and a goodly bag of feathered game were often the result of a half-day's run with a single boat.

Mortimer Halleck, who at this time lived in the fork of the rivers, and at a considerable distance from the rest of us, owned a staunch skiff, which he had himself made, and in it went often alone upon the rivers. It was upon one of these solitary trips that he met with the adventure mentioned.

On a raw afternoon in March, his father had taken Mortimer and his boat on his double horse wagon six miles up stream. At this point there was a great bend in the river, and, by crossing the neck, the water distance to the fork was lengthened to fifteen miles. Mortimer was thus set afloat with his boat, with a long afternoon's run on the river before him.

For several hours the young hunter allowed his boat to drift down with the current, then swollen to an unusual height. His eyes, roving on either hand, were now and then rewarded with the sight of a small brown bunch of fur, resting on a bit of lodged drift. Then followed a quick puff of smoke, and the echoing report from the shot-gun. The troubles of the furry little chap were at an end. The kinks would straighten out of its small humped back, and, as a deft turn of the oars brought the boat alongside, the hunter's hand would reach over the edge, grasp the long, slim tail, and fling the body of the sleek little *musquash* into the boat.

Twice during the afternoon a flock of geese had ventured low down over the drifting boatman, and each time one of the flock had fallen a victim. The others had hurried away in noisy confusion. He had hardly expected to find beaver, yet as the night drew on without a sight of one, he felt a little disappointed. True, he had secured a profitable lot of game: two geese, a mink, and more than a dozen muskrats.

But he wanted to show a beaver with the rest of his bag, and he had about given up his hopes of it when, just as the sun was setting and while he was passing down the mid channel between two long lines of clustering willow thickets, he espied the very object of his desires directly ahead and within easy range.

The animal was rolled up in a rusty brown ball, lying in a snug nest amid the bushy sprouts from an elm stub which projected three or four feet above the water. The tree had been broken off, and leaned out from the summer banks of the river. It had grown, as elm stumps often do, a dense fringe of short, tangled brush about the end of the trunk. Among these sprouts the beaver had fashioned a nest, and was lying curled up, asleep when Mortimer, drifting silently down within short range, raised his gun and shot at it.

But the beaver is a "hard-lived" animal, and, even when shot at such close quarters, will quite frequently flop off its perch into the water, and, clutching with teeth and claws into roots or grass at the bottom, remain there. In that case, the hunter's ammunition is simply wasted.

This had happened more than once in Mortimer's experience, and, fearing that it might happen again, for he saw the beaver floundering heavily in its nest, he brought the boat about in great haste, circled around the stump, and jammed the bow into the sprouts. He then dropped the oars, and sprang forward to secure the game.

His haste was unfortunate; for, though he grasped at the small limbs quickly enough to have held the boat in place if it had not been in motion, his impetus was so great that the unsteady skiff recoiled backward with a force that pitched him over the prow, upon the very top of the stub. He lurched off to one side, and his feet and legs splashed into the water; but he escaped a complete ducking by clenching the top of the trunk with his left arm, while with his right hand he grasped *one foot of the beaver!* And then he glanced around for his boat.

It was gone, and had left him in a most perilous situation. The light skiff, impelled by the force of his

Mortimer looked after it in utter dismay.—Page 58.

fall out of it, had floated back into the current, and was already more than a dozen yards out, moving down stream.

Mortimer looked after it in utter dismay.

It was now too late to make a swim for it; he could never live in that strong, icy current long enough to reach it.

With a few cautious hitches he succeeded in gaining a ticklish seat upon the broken top of the stump, where he maintained himself by resting his feet upon two of the stoutest sprouts. Seated thus, he could feel an unsteady quivering of the trunk, a trembling, wrenching motion, that told, but too plainly, of the powerful force of the flood, and of the uncertain tenure which he possessed on even this comfortless refuge.

The lad was now thoroughly alarmed, and surveyed his surroundings with a growing fear that gained not a ray of hope from the prospect. The situation was truly a grave one.

On all sides was the hurrying flow of the grim, dark waters, which rushed swirling and eddying onward, The current swashed dismally among the slender. swaying willows, on either side; and beyond these, he knew that there was at least three hundred yards of swimming depth before either shore could be reached.

If any one should happen to pass, he could not, from the land, see Mortimer, on account of the willows. The nearest house was three or four miles distant; and a voice could be heard but a little distance, above the swash of the flood and the rush of the cold wind.

Mortimer's parents did not expect him to return until late in the evening, and they would probably make no effort to learn of his whereabouts until after midnight. The night, too, was already growing very cold, with a raw, gusty wind that soughed drearily among the willows; his bare hands and wet feet were fast becoming chilled and numb.

All the desolation, helplessness and misery of the situation were forced upon him by that keen and merciless power of reflection which so often attacks the mind in moments of extreme peril or of sudden disaster.

He saw but too plainly that it was useless to look for rescue before morning, and, clinging there to his bleak and uncertain perch, he felt that he would assuredly chill to death in a few hours.

Looking out into the gloom of the coming dusk, with the long, black, freezing night staring him in the face, tears gathered in the poor fellow's eyes, and a lump of choking misery rose up in his throat. Yet he was a brave fellow, who had never been known to yield an inch before any danger which must be met, when the balance of probabilities was adjusted with any degree of fairness. In this case, the probabilities were all on one side, and that side was against him.

"There just aint any chance for me at all," he groaned, at length. "I'm in a much worse predicament than the beaver and muskrats; for if they do get killed, it's so sudden they don't know it, but I've got to die by inches. I've just got to sit here and freeze a little at a time, till I fall off and finish life by drowning."

A wretched enough prospect! Yet that was the fate which seemed certainly awaiting him. Wet as he was, and already shivering, with no chance for exercise, there seemed little chance of surviving the cold, dismal night.

Sitting in hopeless suffering, he peered about him again and again in the gathering darkness, in the vain hope of discovering something that could give him an atom of comfort. Then, whipping his numbed hands about his shoulders until they tingled, he attempted to remove his soaked and stiffening boots; but, owing to his shaky and uncertain seat, he was baffled in this effort also.

Then, with feet and legs growing every moment more numb, he sat, clinging with one hand to the stump, whipping the other; shouting at intervals, and waiting for—he dared not think what.

An hour passed; then another; dumb, dreary despair had settled upon his mind. Insensibly he fell into a half-frozen stupor. He was beginning to think, in a numb way, that it did not make any particular difference to him what happened now.

An hour or more dragged by thus sluggishly, then a sudden shock, accompanied by a grinding noise, threw him partly off the stump. Instinctively he clutched the sprouts with his chilled fingers, but slid down, expecting to sink in the cold waters.

But he struck something solid and white. It was a large ice-cake, which had come floating down the river and touched the elm stump. The jar of his fall roused the boy; he staggered to his feet, feeling *strange* in his head, and with queer and painful sensations about the arms and shoulders.

He tried to step, but at first it seemed as if his feet must be frozen; yet, after stamping about for a few minutes, they began to lose their feeling of lumpishness and to prickle.

He then sat down upon the ice, and, after a struggle, worked off his boots, squeezed the water from his socks, and chafed and pounded his feet until they felt alive. This done, he got up and looked around; and hope revived within him.

The ice-cake was a large and solid one, twenty feet across at least; and, owing to the falling of the river, it was floating down the centre of the channel. He was, at least, floating toward home; and there was room to stamp about and keep from freezing.

Mortimer's spirits rose with the renewed circulation of the blood. He shouted, beat his arms about his chest, he even danced, the better to warm himself up again.

It seemed to him now that he was being guided by fate. He then became confused in mind—dazed, as it were. In odd vagary, as his ice-raft floated on down the river, he peopled the darkness about him with imaginary foes, and "squared off" at them pugnaciously. His blood warming with this exercise, he began delivering in grandiloquent tones the address which he had declaimed at school, when a voice from the darkness near at hand brought him back to his situation.

"Mortimer!"

"Halloo!" he answered.

"Mortimer, is it *you*?"

"Is that you, father?" cried the young castaway, "have you got a boat?"

"Yes," replied Mr. Halleck; "but we have been alarmed. What has kept—"

"Paddle your skiff this way, father. Here, this way; I'm on a cake of ice."

"On a cake of ice!" cried Mr. Halleck. "I knew you were in some trouble. What has happened? I borrowed Neighbor Wescott's boat, and was going to cross over to see if you were at Morley's with Pete, when I heard your voice."

Mortimer was astonished to find he had already drifted so far.

"How much longer could you have stood it?" Mr. Halleck asked, in tones that trembled a little.

"Not another half-hour," Mortimer declared, and probably he was right.

Next day he succeeded in finding his boat, safely lodged among some willows; but the beaver was missing, having probably been jarred off the nest on the stub by the ice-cake striking against it.

The river had lowered considerably, and Mortimer, while searching for his boat, saw numerous ice-rafts moving down the channel; yet he could not repress a conviction that something more than mere good fortune had directed the ice-cake to touch at his bleak and comfortless perch in the nick of time to save his life.

VI.

THE MYSTERY OF THE VALLEY.

Among the earliest settlers on the Wisconsin river was Robert Wheaton—now one of the wealthiest farmers of the State—who, with his pretty young wife, Jennie, came up into the Winnecon Valley to make a home about the year 1850. There was this difference between the Wheatons and many others of the pioneers here: Robert and Jennie settled there to stay, while too many of the "old Winneconers," yielding to temporary discouragements, drifted away with the ever-moving tide of Westward migration.

Robert, like all "old settlers," greatly delighted to tell of the hardships of those early times, when he and Jennie came to live in the new log-house in one of the Winnecon "pockets," or side valleys between the bluffs.

One midsummer evening, just at twilight, Robert sat milking his cow in the little yard back of his shed, when someone near the fence surprised him with,—

"Good-e'en, Meester W'eäton! Ha' ye seän th' broout baäst yit?"

Robert knew the voice, and looking up, saw "Big Jim" Hodgson, as he was known, leaning his elbow upon the fence. Hodgson was an Englishman, with a large family, and in person an enormous man of six and a half feet in height, who spoke the North of England dialect, in a voice as rough and guttural as the rumbling of a cart-wheel. The Winnecon people among whom he had settled had nick-named him "Big Jim."

He was a brave, good-natured man, but somewhat inclined to be superstitious.

"Hullo, Hodgson!" Robert exclaimed. "What brute are you talking about? I haven't seen any one."

Big Jim explained. There was a strong flavor of hobgoblin belief in his gruff, deep tones, as he related how a strange creature had been seen in the valley roads and along the cow-paths during the past week. One of the Carter girls had seen it up on the "bluff path," between Cat Rock and the Twin Oaks. It was a large, gray, shaggy creature, which, issuing from the brush, had followed the girl as she drove home the cows. She was naturally much terrified, yet she dared not run, and the "broout baäst" had followed her silently, until she had gone past the Twin Oaks, down to the upper end of Carter's rye-patch.

There it had left her and walked off into the woods, and she had rushed home with the cows, and gone to bed in a high fever.

Continuing his account, Big Jim related how, on Sunday evening, the *thing* had followed the Mulrony boys down through the gap road.

"They were on horse-back," he said, "a-coomen' doon on a spaärkin' veesit to Carter's; and the brout baäst 'ad coom oop a-hint their 'orses, 'n' nigh scahed th' seensus oot o' um."

Nor was that all, for last evening, just at dusk, his own little girl, May, had seen it cross the turnip-patch up in the "notch" on the side of the bluff above the house. It went across the patch from one point of timber to the other like a streak of gray light, seeming not to touch the ground with its feet, and "hit warn't nowt loike onythink at all sho 'ad e'er seën."

"W'aüt do Muster W'eäton think o' that, now?"

The question had in its tones a strong touch of exultation, for hadn't Robert Wheaton always "toorned up 's noäse at onythink at all as was onnaäteral?"

Robert laughed, not so much at the information, as at Hodgson's tones. He soon grew sober again, however.

"We must look after that animal, I think, Jim," he said. "I'm inclined to believe, from what you say of the beast and its actions, that we've got a panther sneaking about our neighborhood."

"Mought beä," returned Jim, a little miffed; "but I'se un as b'leäves traäps'll no hoäld un, an' bullut's'll no hoort un," and he walked off toward his home swinging a heavy club as he went.

"Evidence in his hand against the belief in his head," chuckled Robert, who went in with his pail of milk, and told Jennie about the "broout baäst."

"Some stray panther, I expect," he said, in conclusion, "or a big timber-wolf, that's prowling about after pigs and chickens."

A week from the following Sabbath there was "preaching" at the new log school-house. Rob and Jennie attended, and after the service their ears were filled with excited questions, and with remarkable statements about the "broot baste," as the strange creature had already come to be called, this name being an American perversion of Big Jim's North English tongue.

Every one wanted to know whether Robert had yet seen the "thing." Not a few affirmed that they had seen it—always after dark—and it had each time followed silently a little way, and then, as they drew near houses or openings, it had slunk away into the woods. For a fortnight it had followed some one nearly every night. Even the itinerant preacher grew interested.

"Must be a dangerous creature of some kind, Robert," he said, addressing Wheaton; "a wild animal, of course, and you had better trap it."

Nothing, however, could convince Big Jim that the creature was not an uncanny brute; and old Granny Bates, who was born before the Revolution, declared her belief that it was "some creatur' bewitched."

Robert promised to try his hand at trapping it, and went home. In less than a week he had seven large double-spring traps, baited and carefully set at different points in the bluffs where the strange object had been seen.

He had to neglect his work somewhat in order to make the round of these traps; and as they were not disturbed during the whole of this time, the affair proved most annoying to him. At last he grew sceptical about the matter, and took his traps home, declaring that he "wouldn't trap for shadows any longer."

'Somebody," he said to Jennie, "has started a ridiculous story about the creature, and now everybody that sees a dog come out into the road after dark imagines, it's the 'broot baste.' I've found a few fresh wolf-tracks, but there's no sign of any strange animal, that I can see."

But tidings of the "broot baste" did not cease. Scarcely a week passed that some one in the valley or among the bluffs did not have a fresh story to relate of the oddly-behaving creature. It was often seen close to houses, at night-fall, but generally made its appearance to women and children.

As the creature never offered to molest any one, and spared the pigs and chickens, people ceased to fear it and only wondered what it could be.

But Robert remained sceptical as to its existence; and the matter continued to be a mystery.

Late that fall, after the first snow, which came early, there began to be heard strange yelps and cries nearly every night among the hills. These were most "uncarthly noises," the people said who heard them. Robert only laughed at these reports. "Wolves always howl during the first cold snap," he said.

But one night Jennie and he were awakened by what was, in very truth, a most frightful yelping, which came from the bluff, just above their stable. They listened awhile; and Robert was compelled to admit that he "never had heard such an outcry as that from any living creature before."

The cries seemed to be half-way between the quick yelps of a frightened dog and the prolonged howl of a timber-wolf, only more wild, weird and mournful than either of those sounds.

Robert took his gun and went out; but the howling stopped immediately, and it was so dark that he could see nothing.

The next night the creature came and howled in the same place, and earlier in the evening, but it became quiet the moment Robert stepped outside the house. Wheaton's curiosity was fairly aroused.

He tried to find its tracks the next morning; but the snow had now nearly all melted and the ground was frozen again. He said nothing to his neighbors, but determined to outwit and kill the beast, in some way. But though he again set his traps and baited them invitingly with fresh meat, night after night passed and the howling increased, yet the traps remained empty.

Then he tried hiding out in the brush, lying in wait with his gun, but the animal did not appear, and that stratagem failed.

But one night, early in December, the mystery was explained in the most unexpected manner. "Young John," a Winnebago trapper, solved it for them.

Young John, as he was called by the white settlers, was an Indian who, for some offense, was under the ban of his tribe, and who subsisted by trapping and hunting along the Wisconsin.

He could speak broken English, and he evinced a liking for Robert Wheaton, who had taught him many useful things. Hence he often came to Robert's place and slept on the house-floor at night. Generally he ate supper with Robert and Jennie, but he always left before the latter awoke in the morning.

One evening, about three weeks after they had been so disturbed by the howlings of the "broot baste," Young John came to the house, and, as usual, took supper with them, having brought his blanket. prepared to sleep on the floor.

After supper, when Robert had finished his "chores," he sat by the fire with Young John, as they had been in the habit of doing, telling stories, when on a sudden the "broot baste" set up a series of its wild, mournful cries, in the same place on the bluff above the stable.

They had not heard it there for several nights; and

Robert had not yet mentioned the creature's doings to Young John.

On hearing the sounds, the Indian started and listened for a moment most intently, while Robert and Jennie exchanged meaning glances. But Young John's next move surprised them; for after listening for a moment or two, the Indian gave a most expressive guttural grunt of mixed astonishment and satisfaction, then abruptly strode to the door, threw it open, and placing two fingers between his lips, blew a shrill, ear-piercing whistle.

The howlings stopped.

He repeated the whistle, then stalked out into the darkness. Robert and Jennie followed him to the door, and peered out curiously.

It was light enough for them to see the Indian, as he stopped near the corner of the stable; and then they saw a strange, shadowy creature come bounding down the hill and throw itself on the ground, with pitiful whines, at Young John's feet.

He stooped over and seemed to be petting it and talking to it in the Winnebago tongue, for a few seconds. Then he came back to the house; and the creature followed whining and leaping at his heels, until he had nearly reached the door, when it slunk quickly away out of sight again.

Robert and his wife were quite prepared for Young John's announcement, as he came up to the door.

"Me dog," he said. "Me lose um las' spling clossin' liver. Him heap 'fraid white man's."

He made no further comment, and his hearers said nothing. They remembered perfectly well the shy, large, gaunt, grizzled wolf-dog which had always been

with him, and h‌ad always refused ⬛ near the
house, on his pr‌e‌‌‌‌‌‌‌‌‌‌us visits.

Jennie at on‌ce offered the ⬛ ‌victuals, to
feed the anim‌‌‌‌‌al at Young Jo‌h‌‌‌‌‌‌n. ⬛ ‌o, him eat
plenty labbi‌t‌."

The Whe‌‌ ‌d a quiet laugh ⬛ ‌he solution
of the stra‌n‌‌‌‌‌‌‌‌‌‌‌‌‌‌‌‌‌‌ ‌‌r. Next morni‌‌‌‌‌ng ⬛ Indian and
his dog ha‌d‌‌‌‌‌‌‌‌‌‌‌ ‌eared.

The "br‌‌‌‌‌‌‌‌‌‌‌‌‌eakfa‌ste" and its antic‌‌‌‌‌‌s ‌‌re from that
time forth ⬛ ‌s of the past; a‌‌‌‌‌nd ‌‌he neighbors
enjoyed t‌‌‌‌‌‌he expl‌anation as much ⬛ ‌d Robert and
Jennie.

VII.

FOLLOWED.

The most desperate and lawless **men to** be found in the West—I speak from twenty years' experience on the plains—**are the** gamblers, confidence men and robbers who **follow** the "end of track" when a railway is push**ing through** new and unsettled territory.

At every **side-track** a new town springs into existence, so suddenly as to suggest the Western expression "dropped there by a cyclone." At each of these new communities the first-comers are usually men of the kind I have mentioned.

Along the road-bed, wherever a siding is to be laid, a dozen or more big tents, respectively labeled "Saloon," "Dance House," sometimes very appropriately, "Satan's Hole" or the "Devil's Den," are always found set **up** in advance of the arrival of the track-layers.

A certain harvest awaits the owners of these groggeries, as the "railroader," of a certain class, takes his "time" from his foreman at frequent intervals, in order that he may cash his "time check" at the nearest saloon and gambling-place.

He quickly squanders the proceeds of his check in drink and play, or is robbed of them, lies about in a stupid condition for a day or two, and then goes to work again, penniless.

Such a person accepts all the evils of this mode of life with a philosophy that would be commendable if shown under adversity of a different sort. A shirt, pantaloons, shoes, and a slouch hat usually comprise the whole of his possessions, and so long as he can get the means to satisfy a periodic appetite for drunken excitement, he seems to be contented with his lot.

This description of a large class of railroad laborers, it should be distinctly noted, does not apply to the many sober, steady fellows who save the large wages they get, and often settle and become prosperous citizens in the country they have helped to open to civilization.

It is upon the earnings of floating, dissolute wage-workers of the track and grade that the gambler, whisky seller and assassin thrive, and, to secure their plunder, they follow the progress of a new railway like vultures in search of prey.

The day-laborer upon these pioneer roads is not the only victim of the robber and sharper. It is unsafe for any man who visits one of their mushroom towns to let the fact be known that he has a considerable sum of money in his possession.

Yet men who know the nature of the dangers about them sometimes neglect to take proper precaution to insure the safety of money in their charge, and thus the writer allowed himself to be caught, two years ago, in a "snap" that came near ending his career, and that taught him a lesson in caution which he hopes will never again be needed, at least by him.

I was acting as paymaster and chief commissary clerk for a firm of grade contractors upon the Northwestern road, which was then pushing through northern Nebraska into the adjacent territory of Wyoming.

We were doing some heavy grading and rock work,

and with a large force were pushing the work day and night in order to get out of the way of the track, which had then advanced to a point within a day's ride of us.

We had let pay-day slip by without paying the men, and hoped to satisfy them by the issue of time-checks until the track should overtake us, and our money could come to us with little risk on the construction train. But, three or four days after "pay-off" time, some of the men began to grow suspicious and to grumble, and threatened to quit work until their checks were cashed. They were afraid we might somehow slip up on them and they wouldn't get their money.

As we were in desperate need of every available hand, it was necessary that the men should be satisfied. So it was determined that I should go to Chadron, our supply base and banking point, and bring up enough money to pay the men their last month's wages, which amounted to about four thousand dollars.

I decided to go alone. I set out that night on horseback, and I reached the "end of track" at Crawford siding the next morning in time to leave my horse at a neighboring ranch corral and get aboard a supply train which had just unloaded and was now going back.

At Chadron the supply store of the main contractor, a huge, roughly built shed, stood at a side track about forty rods from the main street of the town. Here I was accustomed to order supplies and get drafts for money from the book-keeper from time to time.

That morning, after finishing my business with the supply department, I went to the book-keeper to procure a draft. A crowd of railroad laborers were waiting before his window to get their time-checks cashed, or secure passes to go up or down the road. I noticed that two of these men were better dressed than the others, but thought nothing of the circumstance.

I awaited my turn at the window, and handed the book-keeper a slip of paper on which was written, "Four thousand three hundred and forty-seven dollars and fifty cents, *Pay Roll*—Rodney and Curtis." He made me a draft for the amount named, folded it carelessly, thrust it through the window, and took the receipt which I had just written, and then turned to the next man.

As I left the store I passed the two men whom I had noticed at the window, and it struck me, upon a more attentive view, that they were rather sharpers than workingmen, although I had seen them cash two time-checks and get passes for some point up the road. The construction train did not leave until three o'clock that afternoon, and I lounged upon the shady stoop of the Chadron House watching the passers-by and chatting with the landlord, who was an old acquaintance of mine when I lived in the East. I had a pleasant dinner with him, and after the meal was finished, I walked across the square to Lake & Haley's bank, at the corner of the two principal streets of the town, where I cashed the draft.

The bills which I received I stuffed into various side pockets of my clothes, and stowed a sack of silver change into a small leather "grip" which I carried in my hand.

I heard a locomotive whistle and, turning, walked quickly out of the bank. As I reached the sidewalk I was startled to see the two men who had before attracted my notice step rather hastily away from the sidewalk in front of the bank windows and walk across the street.

I was satisfied that they had watched me as I cashed my draft. My suspicions were thoroughly aroused by this circumstance, and when, an hour later, I stepped into the caboose of the construction train, and discovered the men lounging upon two cracker barrels smoking their pipes, it did not need their evident avoidance of the direct stare I gave them, the moment I entered, to convince me that they were after me.

I had heartily berated myself for not having exercised greater caution while at Chadron. I should have waited until I could see the book-keeper alone before I obtained my check, and should have had my cash made up by the clerk at the bank, and brought to my room at the hotel, as might easily have been done. But it is easy enough, after you have done a foolish thing, to think how much better you might have managed it.

While I sat upon one of the hand benches in the caboose, with my "grip" lying beneath the seat, I considered how I should dodge the two fellows at Crawford. There was no danger that I should be robbed on the train, as there were at least twenty passengers on board. Presently one of the men sauntered up to my seat, sat down by me, and began to talk.

"See?" said he; "you'r with Rodney an' Curtis, aint yeh, one o' their foremen?"

I answered carelessly that I was in their employ.

"Paul 'n' I's goin' up the road lookin' fur a rock job. We're strikers. Could ye hire us, d'ye think?"

"Certainly," said I; "we need more badly, especially

good strikers. Will give you two dollars a day, and you can work a part of the night shift, if you like."

Then, as unconcernedly as I could, I went on to tell him about our work, and directed him how to find our headquarters. I told him I should leave Crawford after breakfast the next morning on horseback, and that he and his partner could undoubtedly find a freight wagon there on which to take passage for our camp.

After some further conversation with the man—a young-looking, wiry, dark-faced fellow—he went over to talk to his "pard," and no doubt they congratulated themselves on his success in throwing me off my guard.

On my arrival at Crawford I went to the company's tent, where food and other supplies brought on the construction trains were stored until they could be shipped forward by wagon to points where our forces were at work. There I explained the situation to the two clerks in charge of the tent, and said that I wished to spend the night with them.

I was armed with a good "six-shooter," and the clerks had each a light Winchester rifle. They said we could guard the money without trouble that night, and it was arranged that I should start for the grading camp at three o'clock the next morning. By leaving at so early an hour I believed that I could baffle pursuit by any robbers who might have conspired to follow me.

My pony—a tough Oregon half-breed—was picketed that evening behind the supply tent, and the clerks and I took turns in sitting on guard at the opening of the tent. I saw nothing of the two "strikers" after we left the train, and no suspicious person approached the tent that night. I shifted the silver from my "grip" into a pair of saddle-bags, and, armed with my revolver and a borrowed Winchester rifle and a belt of cartridges, mounted my pony at three o'clock the next morning to complete my journey.

Day was just breaking when I came to the fork of the trail at Fort Robinson, two miles out from Crawford siding. Both routes led to the grading camp,—one trail lay through White River cañon and the other led to my destination by way of Driftwood. One of these routes I must take, and as the men who were "shadowing" me believed that I would proceed by way of Driftwood I chose the White River cañon route, a rough, new trail that for seventeen miles led through a tumbled, rocky gorge or cañon in the bottom of which rippled merrily the little streamlet that is the beginning of the White River.

I urged my pony forward at a good pace until, after sunrise, I passed a camp of freighters who were preparing their breakfast, and later met several wagons on the move, which relieved the loneliness of my ride and caused me to feel more secure. As the morning was hot and oppressive I now proceeded more slowly.

About half an hour after meeting the freighters I halted at one of the numerous creek crossings, and dismounted to drink and to eat a part of the lunch of crackers and dried beef which I had brought from the commissary tent. As I had no cup I stretched myself out upon the rocks at the edge of the current, and buried my nose in the cool water of the spring-fed stream.

As I lay drinking, with my head just above the water, a distant sound of horses' hoofs struck on my ear. I ceased to drink, listened intently, and soon heard distinctly the noise of horsemen coming rapidly up the cañon.

I sprang to my feet in alarm. My first impulse was to mount my pony and apply the spurs, but as his gait, a racking gallop, was a very slow one, I came to the sudden conclusion to dodge into the brush and let the horsemen, whoever they were, go by. There were a few box alder-trees and several clusters of plum-bush close under the rocks on the right. I grasped the bronco's rein and led him in behind the thickets of thorn and tied him.

I had little time to think or act before the horsemen came up at a gallop; I peered through the leaves as they rattled on, and discovered that there were six riders and that the two strikers were in the lead. They passed my hiding-place without an apparent suspicion that I was concealed there, and, though still much alarmed, I was congratulating myself that I had outwitted them when, just as they rode into the water, my pony lifted up his head and uttered a shrill, inquiring whinny.

The party instantly halted. Every rider turned his face eagerly in my diréction, and a half dozen rifles and revolvers were jerked into readiness for action. My pony whinnied again before I could get a grip upon his muzzle, and I felt that unless some unexpectedly fortunate circumstance intervened I should lose the money and probably my life. The horsemen were determined, villainous-looking men, and as I glanced about I saw they had a great advantage over me. The scattered patches of pine scrub on the steep bare sides of the gorge offered me but little shelter for a retreat, and the

"I thrust the Winchester through the tops of a plum bush and fired."—Page 81.

bushes behind which I stood were but a slight protection against heavy bullets. At the second whinny of my horse the men dismounted and stood behind their animals.

"He's in there, sure," I heard one of them say. "Spread out, boys, an' let's surround them bushes."

Without waiting to hear any more I thrust the Winchester through the tops of a plum bush and fired at their nearest horse, aiming at its body back of the shoulder. The animal went down with a groan, and the man behind it sprang back with a fierce oath.

My only hope now was in swift action and certain aim. A quick motion of the lever re-loaded and cocked my Winchester, and almost before the horse had fallen to the ground I had aimed and fired at the fellow as he turned to run for cover.

He fell, but got up and ran again. Shifting my aim, I opened a rapid fire upon the other horses and men. The robbers returned a few hasty and ineffectual shots, and then scattered in flight. When I had fired the seventeen shots, which emptied my repeating rifle, three horses lay on the borders of the cañon at various distances away, and one man with a broken leg was dragging himself toward the shelter of the creek bank. His companions had fled down the cañon, two on foot and the others on horseback. Three or four of their shots had struck in the brush about me, but none had hit me.

The sudden, fierce determination which had seized upon me, and the swift, effective firing which followed, were as much a surprise to myself as they could have been to the "road agents," who no doubt believed there was more than one shooter behind the bushes that sheltered me. I dared not stop to look after the wounded man, who undoubtedly would have fired at me if I had approached him. Mounting my pony and keeping as much as possible under cover of bushes, I rode my animal at his best speed up the cañon.

About five miles from the scene of the shooting I came upon a grader's camp, and sent some of the men to look after the wounded robber and to secure the saddles of the fallen horses.

I afterwards learned that they got the saddles but could find nothing of the man.

H. H. CUMMACK.

VIII.

OLAF HELGERSON'S PAY.

There were rough times occasionally on the street of Jimtown when big Olaf Helgerson and his friends came in from the Upper Ussawau Lake and made themselves drunk with alcohol and water—not that the water stirred their blood or fired their brains. The Norse settlers of James county generally were of that sober and industrious sort who have borne such a large share in breaking up the great prairies of the Northwest and subduing this big wilderness. But among this people, as among all others, there is more or less "bad blood," only in this case it showed itself boldly and badly in the carousings of Olaf and Gulik Helgerson and their neighbors, the Larsons and Joraegs.

One blustering day in December some dozen years ago they came, a half-dozen of them, to town, and began drinking and soon grew riotous. Up and down the single street of Jimtown they caroused from one saloon to another, pouring down fiery alcohol until their faces flamed and their brains reeled, and they swaggered along the sidewalk kicking and cuffing at each other and threatening everyone else who had the hardihood to meet them.

The town people kept indoors, and no one thought of making an arrest. The town depended for its main support upon the Norse trade, and so a Norse frolic was not to be interfered with.

That afternoon, though, matters "came to a head," and the men came out of their stores and shops and overawed the rough Norwegians, drunk as they were. It happened in this wise: Kneut Halvorsen, a Norse lad living at the Lower Ussawau Lake, came in that afternoon to get mail and some medicine for his mother, who was ailing with rheumatism.

The post-office was kept at "Iliff's" drug store, and as Kneut stepped in there were a number of loafers seated about the big box-stove listening to one of "Old Iliff's" many stories. The old man paused in his narrations and spoke to Kneut.

"Kneut," said he, "Helgerson and his crowd, I s'pose you know, are in town t'day, but mebby ye didn't know that they're drunk as loons and knockin' everybody off the walks? Better git yer mail 'n' go right home."

"Faal," said Kneut, "I ton't alfays pe koin to run afay fou Olaf Helgerson. I kot me yust so koot a ride to keep een te town uss he haf.

"Wall," replied the old man, "I was only givin' ye fair warnin';" and he resumed his story. But his hearers' interest flagged, in view of Kneut's combative spirit, and while Tom Iliff, Jr., was "putting up" a prescription for Mrs. Halvorsen's rheumatism they watched the young Norwegian curiously.

Presently Kneut turned from his purchases and left the store.

"There'll be a fight, sure," said one of the loungers; and he went to one of the front windows and scratched the frost from a pane that he might look out upon the street.

The quarrel of Helgerson with the Halvorsens had long since become common stock in Jimtown's affairs of local interest, and dated back to the first Norse settlement of James county, when Kneut and Gus Halvorsen were lads. It came about by the death of widow Halvorsen's brother, Eric Brakstead, who owed Olaf Helgerson for a yoke of oxen. Eric's claim joined that of his sister, and they lived together and helped each other in improving their new land. Kneut and Gus were old enough to drive teams, and the widow had two yoke of oxen of her own, their interests being kept separate, although they worked often together. In the spring Eric had bought a yoke of steers of Olaf Helgerson, giving a note due in six months, when he expected his wheat harvest would enable him to pay it.

Bad luck followed. In June one of the steers was struck by lightning, grasshoppers came and devoured the growing wheat, and that same autumn poor Eric was taken with typhoid fever and died, leaving his claim to be immediately jumped by the first land-seeker. Helgerson went to the widow with Eric's note and demanded payment when it came due. She informed her neighbor that her poor brother had died owing her money, and that it would be impossible for her to pay his other debts; but she told him there was the other ox left, which, of course, she should expect him to take.

Eric went away in a great rage and immediately brought suit against her. The jury, of course, returned him his ox, but gave her the verdict. From that time on Olaf Helgerson, a wild, rough, passionate fellow, spared no pains to vent his hatred in all ways that he dared against the widow and her boys.

He often threatened Kneut and Gus with terrible threshings, but up till this December day he had never touched either of them. The boys often met their belligerent neighbor upon the road, at the Lutheran church between the lakes, or at other Norse gatherings. However, they had for several years carefully avoided going to town when they knew that Olaf would be there, and as the road from Upper Ussawau to Jimtown ran directly past their door they generally knew when he went or returned. Indeed, they were very likely to know when he came home, for he was nearly always "in liquor" and would shout and curse at them or at the house as he rode by.

But Kneut had grown large and strong as a man, and he had heard Olaf's threats so often that they had become tame; in fact, he had never been afraid of Helgerson, but, knowing the latter's habit of drunken brawling when in town, in keeping away he had acted prudently and in accord with his mother's wishes. Then, too, Olaf, who was a natural leader, had drawn a rough crowd around him who generally shared his drunken bouts and also his quarrels.

Kneut was of a peaceable disposition, a hard-working and honest lad, who desired no quarrel with any one. But this day as he stepped out of "Iliff's" Olaf Helgerson was coming down the opposite side of the street, boisterously drunk and aggressive. He saw Kneut and instantly started across, wading in the snow, wildly swinging his arms and shouting all sorts of threats. Gulik, Olaf's brother, Ole Larsen, and Snell Joraeg followed.

At sight of them and at the word "coward," which they shouted at him, Kneut's young blood boiled. Regardless of consequences he stepped down from the sidewalk and threw off his big knit scarf, his overcoat, and sheep-skin mittens, and with clinched hands awaited them.

"Will you pay me seventy-five dollars?" shouted the drunken Olaf, as he came up; he spoke in the Norse tongue, and flourished his big fists at Kneut's face by way of emphasizing the demand.

"No," replied Kneut; and, fiercely clinching, the two whirled round and round, wrestling and jerking each other about in the snow.

Kneut was strong and sober, and, being a good wrestler, as soon as he "got his head" gave Olaf a sudden trip and flung the tipsy fellow headlong in the snow and then sprang upon him. Then, I suspect, had it not been for his brother, with Ole and Snell, all too brutally tipsy to think of fair play, Olaf Helgerson would have received a sound hammering from Kneut's tough knuckles. But these three now pounced upon Kneut, and, seizing him by the arms and legs, tore him away from Olaf and began dragging him along the street. Olaf staggered to his feet and came after them, swearing loudly at Kneut and threatening dire vengeance.

But the man at Iliff's window, and a number of others at various points on the street, had seen the scuffle, and by that magic which draws people so quickly together at exciting scenes, a crowd gathered and attacked Kneut's tormentors, wrenching them away and driving them from him. The plucky lad was bruised severely in many places, where Olaf had brutally kicked him, but the townsmen were roughly sympathetic, a number of them insisting, in spite of his declaration that he "fan't mooch hoorted," on taking him into "Iliff's" to have his hurts examined, and, if need be, dressed. Others hunted up the constable and assisted the officer to arrest the four drunken fellows and lock them in an old coal-bin, which had been fitted up as a "calaboose."

Kneut's bruises were only black and blue spots on his legs and one arm, and after Tom Iliff had rubbed them well with a patent liniment he went out, got on his horse, and set out for home.

On the road he had time to think coolly—very coolly, if the weather were to be taken into consideration—and in spite of the indignities he had received, he began to regret that he had not walked rapidly off, as he might have done, and get out of the way of Olaf.

"I had no business fighting with drunken brutes like the Helgersons and those other fellows," he thought, "and it will make mother feel badly."

But before reaching home he had something else to think of; the wind suddenly increased to a gale, the clouds thickened and grew dark, and the snow came down in stinging scuds, driving directly in his face. The storm had come on a blizzard, and his horse, a young colt, snorted wildly and shook his head in a protest against facing it. Kneut urged the animal forward, as he had several miles yet to go, and knew from experience that the storm was likely to increase in violence rapidly until midnight or later. Keeping the colt at a stiff trot, and bending forward to break the force of the blinding drift, he managed to keep the road, which, lying in the path of the wind, was in most places swept bare. He had nearly reached the outlet at the foot of Lower Ussawau, when a team with a sleigh attached came dashing up and passed him.

He knew the team at a glance. It was Olaf Helgerson's and Olaf was lying in the bottom of the sleigh, too drunk, probably, to sit up, and one line was dragging. The horses were going at a keen gallop, and, of course, without any control; they ran with their heads low, snorting loudly, and evidently keeping the road by instinct rather than sight. They were young spirited animals, which Olaf had raised and of whose speed he boasted greatly.

"They'll break his drunken neck before he gets home with them," thought Kneut, "or they'll throw him out where he'll freeze to death." This last catastrophe seemed so probable that Kneut, in alarm, forgot, all other feeling toward Olaf Helgerson, and whipped his colt into a run to overtake the sleigh.

He came up with it just at the crossing of the outlet; here, when the sleighing was bad on the road, Helgerson sometimes turned off and went home on an old "hay road" which led through the marshes on the east side of the lake, and here his team, no doubt sheering off to avoid facing the storm directly, took up the old trail which led along the east shore of Lower Ussawau. There were no houses to be met in that direction for several miles, the land being a succession of swamps separated by "hard-head" ridges; the region, several miles in extent each way, was known as Lonesome Township.

Kneut, alarmed at being turned away from the main road even for a moment, ran his colt alongside the runaways, and tried to reach the bridle-rein of the nearest; but the colt he rode, only half-broken, was both "skittish" and unruly, and, try as he might, he could not get the animal near enough to let him grasp a rein or a line. He then made a desperate effort to get in front of the flying horses and stop them; but again the unruly colt, frantic with his lashing and the pelting of

He then made a desperate effort to get in front of the flying horses.—Page 89

the storm, proved intractable, and would only rear and plunge in an effort to keep out of the way of the team.

Failing in this attempt Kneut reined up for a moment, half tempted to let the team go with its helpless master, trusting their instinct to get him home safely. But no, he could not do that. Olaf was lying there like a log, with his big buffalo coat on and also a robe thrown partly over him; but even if he were not freezing already another half-hour of such stupor in a biting storm, Kneut reasoned, would surely finish him.

The tipsy fellow had no doubt broken away from his jail, or given bail, and had started for home, trusting to his horses to take him through, as they had been known to do on two or three occasions. No; plainly Kneut could not desert him in this howling storm, with all that waste of country to traverse and no guide but the instinct of dumb brutes.

All this came to the brave lad much more quickly than I have written it, and no doubt in different form, but, at any rate, he urged his colt forward in the trail of the sleigh, determined to follow until a chance offered for gaining control of the team.

Several times he attempted to ride alongside, with the purpose of flinging himself out of the saddle and into the sleigh-box, but the unmanageable colt each time foiled him by plunging and floundering and falling back in the rear.

Presently, striking a long flat where the ground had been burned bare by the fall fires, and the covering of snow was light, Olaf's team quickened their pace to a stiff run, and then for some minutes there followed a race in which Kneut could barely keep in sight of the runaways. The old hay-road had disappeared entirely, and the storm was growing thicker every moment. The snow whistled across, cutting Kneut's cheek as he bent forward and filling space with a thick white dust through which he had to strain his sight to penetrate even the distance of a few rods.

It was a perilous, a despairing chase ; no road left, the lake-shore out of sight, the direction no longer certain, night coming on, and the furious blizzard growing thicker and colder each moment. Even should the horses hold out, and all survive until the surrounding settlement could be reached, darkness must first overtake them, and through that blinding drift of snow no light could be seen at a hopeful distance.

All this Kneut realized and was terribly frightened ; but he pressed on heroically, digging his heels into the colt's ribs and urging it on with his voice and managing to keep the sleigh and the flying team in sight. The effort kept him warm. Suddenly the ground grew rough and boggy and the colt stumbled and fell, pitching Kneut over its head and wedging him between two hummocks so tightly that it took him some seconds to extricate himself. He had clutched the bridle-rein tightly, so tightly that it had broken at the buckle, and as he struggled finally to his feet he still held the long end in his hand while the colt snorted and floundered about him among the bogs and snow.

Kneut hastily rebuckled the rein and mounted. He could no longer see the sleigh, but there was still the trail, though fast filling up, where the plunging team had wallowed through the snow amid the bogs. He followed for a few rods and came within sight of an object which proved to be the sleigh without the horses ; the beam of the front "bob" had struck solidly against a frozen hummock and the runner had broken, leaving the team free of burden.

Kneut hastily tumbled off his horse, tied its halter to a ring in the end rod of the sleigh-box, and hurried around to Olaf, who lay motionless in a kind of heap where he had been thrown by the jolt into the front end of the box.

A moment's examination proved that Helgerson was alive and not yet badly chilled, for his face was flushed and he was actually snoring in a drunken stupor of sleep. Kneut shook him roughly, and even pounded him in an effort to arouse, but could only get him to fling his arms about and mumble drunkenly while the snow pelted down in his face.

Kneut, finding it impossible to get him awake, ceased trying, and looked about in desperation to see what, if any thing, might be done to save him from freezing to death—as he must soon, exposed in this helpless condition.

The Norse lad did not stop to think of his own perilous situation. A glance about him discovered the fact that the sleigh had lodged at the edge of a slough and that a dense growth of tall rushes was in sight a few yards distant. They had been too green to burn when the early fall fire had swept across them, and it was in such rush brake, he remembered, that, years before, the deer used to take refuge from the winter's cold and storms.

His plan was formed at once, and, going to his colt he deliberately stripped it of saddle and bridle and turned it loose. "Save yourself if you can, Jan," said he, and the animal plunged out of sight while he was speaking.

Kneut then turned his attention to Olaf. He wrapped the buffalo-robe and blanket which lay in the bottom of the sleigh-box about the stupid man, rolling him in them; then, seizing him about the waist, lifted his limp body out of the sleigh. Then, with a mighty effort, he tugged his big enemy forward, dragging Olaf's long legs among the bogs, through the snow and in among the rushes. He pushed on, puffing and even sweating with exertion, until he had reached a point within the brake where the thicket became so dense that he could no longer get on and carry his burden. Then he dropped Olaf, and with his hands broke down the rushes in front, making a path some rods further. Here he could scarcely feel the wind, and, thankful enough to have found such fortunate shelter, went back and dragged the stupid Helgerson to it. Then, clearing away a little spot and piling the rushes at one edge for fire-wood, he opened Helgerson's big coat and searched the pockets of his inside garments, and luckily, with a pipe and a package of tobacco, in one of them was a box of matches. Then, rolling Olaf up in his robe and blanket again, he got down over the pile of rushes and managed to light them.

And now began a strange and wearisome night vigil.

Darkness was already coming on, and Kneut began industriously breaking rushes for fuel. He broke them upon the windward side and threw them in heaps upon the fire. An armful of them would not burn three minutes, but that made no difference; the fire must be kept going, and undauntedly he worked on for hours and hours.

He had laid Olaf as close to the blaze as he dared,

and occasionally he turned his huge bundle over that the heat might get a chance at both sides.

Once and a while he pounded Helgerson vigorously and then listened to his breathing, but he could only spare a moment in each effort to awake the sleeper, as the fire had to be kept going at all hazards.

The circle of open space in front of the blaze grew wider as Kneut broke the rushes and threw them on. They were so thick, though, that an armful could be gathered without stepping out of his tracks. Steadily he worked, while the storm whistled and howled about his head, and the swaying rushes alternated with the driving snow in dealing him stinging cuts upon the face.

It was nearly morning when Olaf, after a pounding, came to himself, and, after rubbing his eyes and mumbling in a growling voice for a bit, sat up before the fire. Curiously and half-dazedly he watched Kneut coming and going at the fire.

Presently Kneut threw on an extra large armful and stopped in front of Olaf.

"Halloo, Olaf Helgerson!" he shouted. "Do you know where you are?"

Olaf gazed at him earnestly for a minute.

"You are Kneut Halvorsen," he said. "How came we here?"

And then, while feeding the flame lightly with a fresh bundle of rushes, Kneut told his story.

When he had finished Olaf staggered to his feet and threw his arms about Kneut.

"Kneut, Kneut?" he burst out, hugging the lad close to him, "I've got my pay! I've got my pay!" And the big rough fellow, in his wonder and gratitude, wept like a child, while Kneut supported his unsteady limbs. He had sobered suddenly and thoroughly, and after Kneut had helped to walk him about a bit gained the use of his limbs, and for the balance of the night helped Kneut to keep the fire going.

While walking about Olaf told how he remembered rushing against the door of the "calaboose," breaking it down and running for his sleigh, but he could remember nothing further.

Morning came soon, and though it was still storming hard, the air was not so filled with snow as it had been, and they managed, by rightly calculating the direction of the wind, to gain the lake shore, and from that point it was an easy matter to find the way around to Kneut's home, just above Elk Grove Point. Widow Halvorsen's surprise was as great as her anxiety had been; and, when her son and her late enemy had recounted their story while warming themselves at the fire, her thankfulness was greatly increased to know that the night's adventure had made them friends as well as brought them safe out of the storm.

By almost a miracle of instinct or luck Olaf's horses reached his house in safety and found their way into his cattle-shed, where they spent the night among the cows; but Kneut's colt perished in the blizzard, and was found afterwards some five miles east of the lakes. It had, no doubt, run until exhausted, and then lain down to freeze.

Olaf replaced Kneut's loss with another horse, insisting that even then he was, and always would be, Kneut's debtor, and since that night his neighbors declare that he has been a good neighbor and a decent man.

IX.

A WILD NIGHT-RIDE.

At nine o'clock one September evening in 1876 I took the coach which left Custer City—or Custer Village, for the town consisted of twenty or thirty log structures—to go to Sidney, Nebraska. A coach, I suppose it should be called, though on the plains this vehicle, which has the driver's seat on the same level as the passengers' seats, is called a "hack."

I had gone to the "Hills" to engage in mining, but after four months of prospecting had decided to open a general supply-store at the new town of Deadwood, and was on my way to Omaha to purchase goods for the venture.

A tin lamp, fastened in one corner of the "hack," discovered to me two passengers within as I entered and took my seat. One was an old gentleman, apparently weak and ill, for, although it was not a cold night, he was muffled in a coarse, heavy ulster overcoat. Moreover, so much of his face as I could see between a gray beard which almost covered it and the rim of a slouch hat was pale and thin, and the eyes looked sunken and unnatural. At least, so it struck me at a cursory glance.

The other passenger was a young fellow of twenty-two or twenty-three years, I judged, decidedly dandified in his dress for that region. He wore a stiff hat and a stand-up collar encircled by a neat tie, and had on a dark suit, evidently custom-made, which was an unusual "get-up" for that region, and one which at once aroused my suspicion, for the only persons I had seen about the mining towns dressed in anything like that fashion were gamblers, a class of men I had made it a point to avoid.

Just before setting out the driver came to the side of the vehicle, thrust in a light Winchester carbine, and placed it between my knees.

"I see you didn't have no gun," said he, "an' I keep a couple of extra ones fer sech."

That was all. No further explanation was necessary in those days.

I took charge of the weapon, although I was as little expert in its use as I was in handling the Smith & Wesson in my hip-pocket, which, indeed, I had never yet discharged.

I knew enough of life in the mines to know that the "bad man with a gun" is usually the man who gets into difficulty rather than the peaceful and unarmed citizen; but a stage-ride from Custer to Sidney at that time was a trip not altogether likely to be without its adventures, and for once I regretted my unfamiliarity with "shooting irons."

It occurred to me that if we were "jumped by road agents," as the phrase went, the freebooters of the route would have little to fear from the occupants of the hack, whether they got much money or not.

There were usually valuables of some sort in the iron box under the driver's seat.

The young man who sat opposite me had a carbine across his lap, but I fancied he knew even less of its use than I did. As we started he sat, without noticing me, twirling a slight mustache and humming a tune.

"A fresh gamester, if one at all," I said to myself upon a second look at him.

The old man had no arms in sight. The driver no doubt regarded him as out of the fight at any event.

As we rolled on up into Buffalo Gap I had a few words of conversation with my companions. I learned that the elder was an Iowa farmer who had come out to see what he could do in the new mines, but he had been ill with mountain fever, and afterward attacked by rheumatism, so that he had been forced to abandon his projects and return to the East. He spoke freely, and in the careless English of Western men.

The young fellow said he was from New York. "Neh Yawk," he pronounced it. He was, he said, a student of mining engineering, but he did not mention what his business had been in that region; but that was not strange, for we could not talk much. A jolting stage bowling over a rough country at eight miles an hour does not give the best opportunity for conversation.

I soon became sleepy, and leaning back in my corner, took such momentary cat-naps as the nature of the road permitted. At eleven o'clock we made a brief halt at a temporary stage station, where the driver's four-in hand team was exchanged for fresh horses.

I peeped out, and got a glimpse of the teams, of two men with a lantern, of a low structure of sod or adobe faintly outlined, and of the black side of a pine-covered mountain beyond. The night was quite dark, with floating clouds and no moon. It became somewhat lighter as we passed out of the gap a little later, as I noted through a crack in the swaying "flap" opposite.

The road was now smoother, and I settled back in

my corner, as my companions had done, to get a little solid sleep if possible. I dozed off for a time, but was awakened by the groaning of the old man beside me. He seemed to be in great pain, and writhed about nervously. I asked him what was the trouble. He replied that the rheumatism in his legs was nearly killing him.

"I wisht the driver'd let me aout when we git t' th' nex' crick. He'll water likely, 'n' I've jest got t' stretch my legs er die. Ye see I'm troubled with cramp rheumatism, an' th' ain't no room in hyer t' get the cramp out o' my legs."

I told him I would speak to the driver when we halted, a few minutes later, at the bank of a stream— White River, I believe. I thrust my head out at the side, and asked that the old gentleman might be let out for a moment to stretch his legs.

"All right!" said the driver, as he clambered down from his own seat. "I'm goin' ter oncheck 'n' let the hosses take a pull at th' drink."

I then helped the old man to dismount, steadying him by the arm as he got down. He seemed to have a good deal of difficulty in alighting, and groaned in a most lugubrious fashion. The flap swung to after him, as I had unbuttoned it all around to let him out. The young man opposite me lay curled up on his seat, but I could see that his eyes were wide open, and that he was eying me with a sharp, keen glance. My eyes probably responded when they fell upon his, for he straightened up in an alert fashion, and leaned toward me.

"Say," he whispered, "do you think that old chap's all right? Strikes me that groaning of his was put on. What dy'e think?"

The question startled me no less than the young fellow's manner, and I was about to make some reply when a gun or pistol shot rang in our ears, followed by a yell either of pain or surprise, and a lurch of the hack threw me forward against my companion's knees.

Either the shot or the yell had startled our team, and we went down the bank and into the stream with a lunge. I heard shots—one, two, three—as we splashed through the water. Then more yells, loud and fierce.

My notion of what had happened or was happening was confused for a moment, and then I saw my comrade—for the light still burned—crawling through to the driver's seat as we went careening up the opposite bank.

A second later he had gathered the lines, which were tied in front, and while he held them with one hand he grasped a front rib of the hack with the other. Then he leaned out and glanced back.

Luckily the horses, which were going at a gallop— they were animals which needed no urging—kept to the road, and the cool-headed young fellow was not pitched out.

"There's a lot of 'em," he shouted in at me a moment later. "I can just see four or five getting onto their horses. They've killed the driver, I guess, and after us now!"

With that he gathered up the long-lashed whip, which lay in the boot, and dropping upon his knees began yelling and laying the whip upon the team.

In a moment we were going at a fearful pace, and despite the excitement and fright of the moment I noticed that our four horses came to hand and ran with a steady, even gait which did credit to the young man's driving.

"Get ready for 'em now!" he screamed back at me; "they'll be down on us in a minute. Open the back flap 'n' pour it into 'em with your guns, and when they're empty get mine under the seat!"

He was my captain as well as driver, and I obeyed instinctively, for I certainly had formed no plan of defense or action on my own account.

I managed to unbutton and roll up the leather behind, and peering out, on my knees before the back seat, I saw that we were indeed followed. It was light enough to distinguish objects dimly at a hundred yards, and there were at least five horsemen in our rear, tearing along at the top of their animals' speed. Knowing that they were within rifle-shot I opened fire on them over the seat. I worked the lever of my gun as rapidly as I could, but made awkward business of it. Presently I got a shell stuck, and began trying to get it out. In the meantime our pursuers were gaining with every second.

They were within fifty yards before I could get out my shell and I was too excited to think of using another gun. Suddenly the light in the hack went out, and a hand upon my shoulder jerked me backward. Then a voice yelled in my ear:

"Let me get at them! Load the guns for me, 'n' let the team go. We might's well smash as be riddled by bullets. Here, here's two boxes of cartridges!"

I dropped back to the other seat and gave place to him. He threw his carbines over the back of the hind seat and began firing.

Crack! crack! crack! It seemed to me that a

steady stream of fire poured out of the back of the stage, and before I had filled the magazine of my gun, his was empty. He snatched mine, however, and thrust his own back at me.

Loading was awkward business at first, as I had to feel for the feeder, but I managed soon to thrust them into my gun as fast as he could work the lever of his own. The men, whoever and whatever they were, rode up to within twenty-five or thirty yards, and, spreading out, opened fire on us.

"Keep close down in the bottom!" shouted my comrade, as he kept on with his firing.

The "road agents" did not come nearer, evidently fearing too great exposure to the stream of shots from the hack, and my courage rose to something near the level of my companion's. I caught glimpses, as I glanced up now and then, of a plunging horse-man with shadowy, outstretched arm, from which flashed blaze after blaze of light.

All at once we began descending into a gulley, and the hack bounced from side to side so violently that it was impossible for us to do anything but cling to the sides of the box.

"It's all right!" rang my companion's voice in my ear, shortly after we had begun the descent; "they've quit. They can't ride along the side of the gulch, and daren't follow straight behind. There's a stage ranch below, too. I remember the road."

Sure enough, the men had dropped back, and the shots ceased. My cool, brave comrade now clambered over me, and in some way got into the front seat of the jumping coach. A moment later I noticed that we were slowing up and running more steadily. Five minutes more we halted, what was left of us, safe and sound in front of a stage station.

Our story was soon told, our horses exchanged and a fresh driver, doubly armed, put with us. Such little accidents did not stop stages in those parts.

There was no danger, they told us, from that same gang. The three men who were left promised to go immediately and look after our other driver.

It was only the darkness and the motion of the vehicle and horses that had saved us from being hit.

We found several bullet marks about the coach next morning; one of them, well aimed, had gone through the back seat at an angle and into the front, and must have passed directly between us. My respect for my young companion was greatly raised by the events of that night, and was further increased by an after acquaintance which discovered his real modesty and worth.

On my return to the "Hills," I learned that our driver had been picked up at the crossing of the creek, badly wounded, and also that the brave fellow had yelled to the team to go the very second he was hit. He had been carried to Sidney. As to the rheumatic old man, he was, of course, a rascal in league with the band who had attacked us.

X.

CARLEN AND HIS COMET.

Several years ago, if one had been traveling through Lake Township, in a county of eastern Dakota, and had inquired who was its best known and most reputable citizen, the answer in almost every case would have been Emmet Carlen, and almost any settler could have pointed out on the level prairie, from his own door, the house and buildings of the young Norwegian upon the crest of "Tip-Top Knoll," at the head of Rush Lake.

Emmet began life in Lake Township as many other Norsemen in many other regions of our New West have done, with no possessions save a change of clothing; but, at the end of a few years, he had, by his thrift and industry, secured and improved a new farm, and placed himself on the sure road to comfort and plenty.

At the time of which I write, however, it was not so much his thrift that made him a marked man, but a certain daring, cool-headedness which he had always displayed when courage and intrepidity were demanded

Once, at his own great peril, he had carried food and extra clothing to a school-teacher and a half-dozen small children who were confined in a little school-house, nearly a mile from any habitation, by one of the fiercest blizzards ever known in that region. This happened during the first year of his stay there, and while he was working for his board and attending school with the little ones whose lives he saved.

Strangely enough, he was again to figure as the rescuer of two of these same children from another sweeping storm, one even more terrible than the dreaded blizzard, a storm of fire, as it swept over the tall, dry grass of the unbroken prairie.

To this exploit, however, there was another party, Emmet's big steer, " Comet," without whose aid, indeed, the children must have perished.

This animal was quite as noteworthy as his master. "Comet" was a huge, long-legged, long-horned steer. For two years Emmet had only his help in plowing and cultivating the "Tip-Top" homestead, except that the breaking of sod was done by hired "breakers."

The young Norseman hitched his steer to a heavy cart, and drove him to market at the small but ambitious town of Boomerang, eight miles distant. In winter, when snow fell and the roads were good, a light sled took the place of the cart.

Before the sled Comet soon gained a local reputation for speed upon the road. His gait was a steady, long-stepping trot, like that of an elk, and nearly as swift. At any rate, it was soon an admitted fact that there were no horses in the neighborhood that could pass Comet in a trotting-match. This was abundantly proved by many races along the road to town and back, where the drivers of the teams or single horses had tried and failed to "go by" the fleet steer.

Comet had taken his name from a former owner, and it was given him because of his wonderful speed and a habit of flying his long tail as a horizontal streamer while "cutting" away from the herd and the herder's pony. The owner was willing to sell the animal cheap, because he was unruly and hard to break. Emmet heard of the chance to buy, and bethought him of the plan, often adopted in Norway, of driving oxen singly.

But he had no ready money. Although he had strong objections to running into debt, he did so now, and obtained Comet by giving his note for twenty dollars. Then, having fashioned a yoke and harness of the Norse pattern, he set to work with characteristic patience and kindness to bring the big, headstrong animal "under the yoke."

His success, though won after a hard struggle, was complete, and, in a few weeks Comet, hitched to a vehicle made from two wheels of an old wagon, with Emmet seated upon the axle, was driven to Boomerang. There the young fellow bought a few boards at the lumber yard, nailed together a rough box, secured it by bolts and braces to the axle which had served him for a seat, and rode home in triumph.

That autumn Emmet bought a small ten-inch stirring plough, and turned over ten acres of sod. The steer pulled the implement with ease after a short training.

The next year another ten acres was broken upon the homestead, and Comet was still sufficient for all Emmet's purposes. It was in October of this year that the event which is the subject of this narrative occurred.

Emmet was ploughing. The day was one of those common to that season in new prairie regions, smoky, with a strong northwest wind smelling of burned grass, a fine dust of cinders sifting down, and sun shining through smoke and dust with a dull red glare. But as Emmet had sometime before burned a broad "fire break' around his shanty, grain and haystacks, he noted these evidences of raging fires without uneasiness. They came at some time every autumn.

It was about the middle of the afternoon that little

Jake and Lib Walker came into his field, bringing some grain bags which Emmet had lent their father to use during his threshing the week before.

Walker lived at the foot of Rush Lake, about a mile from the school house, where the young Norwegians had taken lessons in English, and these little fellows, Jake and Lib, had been his schoolmates when the "big blizzard" came, cutting them off suddenly from home and imperilling their lives.

"Hal-lo, Yakie; hal-lo, Libbie! You a koot fays from home, aint it?" was Emmet's greeting as the lads came up, each staggering under a back-load of sacks.

"We've been a good deal further'n this more'n once," said Jake, "and we've got to go clear round the lake 'n' drive the cows home yit to-night. They're away over yonder," pointing across the lake, "where the wild rice grows 'long the edge, and pa's gone to town."

"Sit you ride town on t'em packs t'ere," said Emmet, "unt rest yo' lecks, unt I feel let Comet rest, too. I did tink meppe as I coot feenish tot bloughin' py night-time put I ton't know off I ken to ut."

And then, seated on the plough-beam, he talked pleasantly with the boys for a few minutes, then telling them that he would carry the sacks to the house when he turned out, bade them "look out unt not ket lost een t'em tall krasses,"—tall grass—as they trudged sturdily away toward the upper end of the lake.

The lads had been gone from the field about half an hour when Emmet noted with alarm that the smoke which had pervaded the air all day had thickened, until now the sun was almost clouded over, showing only a dull red disk. The smell of burning grass had grown more pungent.

His fears were aroused wholly on account of the two boys who had gone to the other side of the lake. The field in which he was at work lay upon the south side of the hill upon which his shanty stood, shutting off the view to north and west, from whence the wind was blowing.

He unhitched Comet at once, and drove him at a trot to the top of the hill.

No sooner had he reached the crest than he saw cause enough for alarm. Not two miles away to the northwest dense volumes of smoke were rising and rolling forward over a broad stretch of prairie. A big prairie fire was sweeping down at a tremendous rate of speed, the "head fire" lining out directly toward the head of the lake.

What could he do to save those two boys? was the young Norwegian's first thought. They must be even at that moment, he thought, well round the head of the lake, wading through the tall grass of the flat. There was no bank to the lake upon that side; wild rice and tall rushes grew far out into the water, and this swamp growth would burn to its very edge. He could not race with the fire on foot, and he doubted if even a horse would be able to outstrip it, but he instantly resolved to make the trial with Comet.

He had frequently ridden the big fellow, who had become as docile and obedient as a dog, to and from the field, hawing and geeing him about at will. Now, if possible, he would ride the fleet-footed steed to some purpose. To throw off the yoke and harness, tie a rope around the animal's body to cling to, and another to either horn to serve as reins, was the work of a minute; then, whip in hand, Emmet mounted and was off.

Comet, feeling a few stinging blows of the whip, broke away at his swiftest trot. Although his gait had more than once defied the best trotters of the settlement, the big steer could hold it with ease for a length of time that seemed incredible. In fact, as had been proved when Comet ran wild among the settlement herds, the animal was as nearly tireless as flesh and blood could be.

But it was a rough ride, and Emmet was obliged to cling tightly with one hand to the girth-rope, while managing reins and whip with the other.

The whip, however, was not needed, and the rider had only to yell "Hi! Hi!" to keep the steer flying at his best gait. With head up and tail streaming, Comet rounded the point of the lake, some half-mile from the knoll cabin, just as the "head fire" reached the upper end of the flat which lay to west and north of the lake.

That "head fire" was now not a mile distant, and was coming directly down the flat which followed the southeast trend of the lake.

The smoke had grown so thick that Emmet could only see a few hundred feet ahead, but he kept well within sight of the lake shore, knowing that the boys could not have gone far down as yet, and that they were not likely to wander far from the lake's edge, for fear of getting lost. Their cattle, too, would be found along shore, feeding upon the rice-heads.

"Hi! Hi! Hi!"

Away they tore through the high grass, across ditches, over rough, boggy spots, the rider getting a terrible pounding, the steer possessed of but one instinct, it seemed—to respond to those sharp yells with the utmost possible strides of his long, fleet legs.

The fire meanwhile was gaining every moment, in spite of his tremendous exertion. Emmet could see that the smoke closed in thicker, and feel that the air was growing hot and oppressive.

But suddenly two little dark objects appeared a few yards ahead, bobbing above the waving grass.

Emmet gave a shout of delight; it was the black heads of Jake and Lib, nodding as they ran. Their hats were off, and they were running as fast as the wilderness of grass would let them.

In an instant Comet was alongside, and, with a few sharp whoas and a hard pull at the reins, Emmet managed to stop him but a few yards in front of the boys.

They ran to him with eager shouts, their fright turned to joy at the sight of him. But without waiting to answer them he leaned forward, caught Lib by the arm, and swung him up in front, then helped Jake to scramble on behind.

"Hank tight to me, Yake," he said; then, throwing an arm around Lib and grasping the rope, he dug his heels into Comet's ribs, and with a shrill "Hi! Hi!" set the steer off again at a swinging pace.

The crackle and roar of the fire could plainly be heard as they started, and Comet, either objecting to his additional burden or uneasy at the smell and the roar of the fire, began snorting and throwing his head on either side ominously.

Emmet feared that the steer would become unmanageable, and as a last resort, determined to run him into the lake and make a swim for it. Somewhere not far below, he knew there was an arm of the lake about one hundred yards wide, extending out a considerable distance into the flat, and this arm, or bayou, he had hoped to reach.

He knew that Comet would not hesitate an instant to plunge into it and swim,—the steer had been known

"Hank tight to me, Yake."—Page 111.

to swim clear across the lake itself,—and once upon the other side, he could soon make his little party safe.

Suddenly the smoke lifted, and he ventured a glance backward. The sight was appalling! The smoke, driven upward by the rush of heated air, was flying above their heads, leaving the jumping flames in plain view.

The head fire was not a quarter-mile distant, Emmet judged, and was bearing down on them with terrible speed, the flames shooting higher than he had ever seen them rise before.

Little Jake and Lib clung to him without a word, while Comet threw his head about and snorted more violently than before.

But suddenly there was a strip of water before them; the arm of the lake had been reached. A moment more, and they were into it with a splash, and Comet was swimming with his heavy burden and carrying it more easily than he had been able to bear it upon land; but his body sank until the water came up to Jake's waist, and nothing but the nose and horns of the steer could be seen.

But swimming was much slower work than running had been, and by the time the opposite shore was reached the fire was already roaring at the other edge.

Emmet leaped off into the edge of the water, and pulled Jake and Lib with him.

"Here!" he shouted, giving them the ropes. "Hank tite to 'im; ton't let 'im loose off you can hold to 'im. You yust so safe as to home now."

They obeyed manfully, and Emmet, drawing a match-box from his vest pocket, dropped upon his knees at the nearest dry place, and, lighting a match, held his hat over it until the flame had touched the blades of grass which he bent toward it; then he stepped back into the water and took charge of the steer again.

The flames on the other side had now reached the

water's edge, and bunches of burning grass were blown toward them.

For an instant the heat was intense, almost scorching. Great tongues of angry flame lapped over among the waters and reached out toward them. *Then, with a final cracking *whish!* they died out, leaving a black, smoking surface beyond.

The fire swept on around the bayou, but meanwhile Emmet's small blaze sprang up and stretched away, gathering force and speed as it swept a wider space.

Comet took things quietly after his swim, which had cooled his skin, and his dripping coat of hair served to protect him from the violent heat which reigned for a moment.

"Fäll," said Emmet, when the coast was clear, "Fäll, little poys, ve kin ko to you' house now."

Walker's house was only a mile distant, but they reached it long after the fire had passed, and found that Mrs. Walker had been nearly wild about her boys until she saw them coming.

"I might have known you'd save 'em," she said to Emmet, while grateful tears ran down her face, as she listened to the story of their escape. Their cattle had taken fright and come home about an hour before.

XI.

CAUGHT IN A BLIZZARD.

The tremendous hurricane of snow and wind which swept over our great, level Northwest in January, 1888, was accompanied by incidents tragic, thrilling and heroic, that will no doubt become a part of the history of the vast region over which the storm swept.

In northwestern Iowa the blizzard descended with a suddenness and fury which made the early settlers shudder as they thought of the barren, unprotected prairies of fifteen or twenty years before. "If 'twasn't for our maple and cottonwood groves and big fields of cornstalks," said they, " wouldn't we ketch it?"

Happily, we had these protections, and suffered neither loss of life nor great inconvenience, though we complained more or less because our daily mails were cut off and our freights delayed even for a short period. But really our most important grievance when we are visited by these occasional fierce storms in winter is the stoppage of hay hauling, pressing and shipping, which is our chief industry at that season.

It was in connection with hay hauling in one of our marshy, unsettled townships that there occurred an incident of extreme peril, of fortitude and intelligent exercise of the faculties amid great danger, which, at the time it came to light, was almost lost sight of in our interest in the widespread calamities which fell upon our unprepared neighbors on the more newly settled prairies of the North and West.

The little railway station of Dupont, in one of the thinly settled districts, was built entirely in the interests of the hay-pressing business, for which the uninhabited flats of Lowland and Gull Lake townships furnish thousands of tons of grass.

The land in these townships is mostly owned by Eastern speculators, who obtained it cheaply under the first Entry Laws and the Swamp Land Act. Although much of it is excellent farm land, these owners have held the price so high as to keep off the actual settlers entirely. This they have been able to do by renting the lands for pasturage and haymaking, and getting enough out of the rent to pay the taxes, and even in some cases a fair interest on the first investment, which was extremely small.

Over this tract, a dozen miles in extent, as far back from the railway as hay can be hauled with profit, are scattered every summer the camps of the haymakers, and the low ricks or "stacks" grow and accumulate until they dot the prairie so thickly as to become for the time the distinguishing feature of the landscape.

There are at the station large hay barns, containing steam presses, to which, from September until April, the hay is hauled, stowed and baled, ready for shipment.

Among those who were hauling hay at the time of the great storm were Dick Jordan and his small brother Orr—named after an Iowa statesman—a little fellow, too young to attend school regularly, who went along on pleasant days to tramp down the hay in the frame of the big rack.

It had been pleasant enough for Orr to go on every trip that week up to the night of the blizzard, and the day was so warm and fine that Dick's sisters, Jeanie and Carrie, younger than himself but older than Orr, obtained the permission of their teacher to go home at recess, in order that they might go with their brothers for a ride to the hay-field. Their mother had promised that they should go upon the first warm day after sleighing came.

They arrived at the house just as Dick and Orr drove up for a lunch, before going after their last load for the day, and, as it would be dark before they could get back, the girls, too, got each a slice of bread and cold meat to munch on the road.

Dick spread two heavy horse-blankets, which were always carried in winter to throw over his horses when standing, upon one of the bottom boards of the rack, and seated Jeanie and Carrie upon them. Then, little dreaming what was before them, the brothers and sisters drove swiftly out upon a new sleigh road, which led them for several miles over a prairie almost as level as a barn floor.

The haystacks were reached, and while the boys worked at their loading, the little girls raced about, tumbled in the hay, or rolled snowballs as they pleased.

The load of hay was taken from the bottom of a stack around which the snow had drifted, thawed and frozen until much of the outside hay had to be cut loose with an axe or freed with a shovel, both of which implements Dick carried for that purpose. It took much longer than usual to load upon this occasion, and evening was already drawing on when finally the little girls were helped upon the load and the team was turned toward home.

It had been mild and thawing all day, so mild,

indeed, that Dick had feared that this would be their last trip with a sleigh until snow should come again; but as he climbed upon the load to start for home, he noticed that a heavy gray bank had formed across the western sky, and that it seemed to be growing thick overhead. The air had suddenly become rather chilly.

He told his brother and sisters that it would snow before they got home, and that they had better "cuddle down" in the hay and throw the horse-blankets over their laps. He drove forward for a few minutes, urging the horses to a half-trot, and uneasily glancing toward the dense gray bank, which rapidly overcast the west and north, and threw a gloom and cold in advance, as it approached.

The darkness came on rapidly, and soon the roar of a high wind broke upon Dick's ears.

"It's a blizzard!" he thought, with alarm, for he had been bred upon the Northwest Prairies, and knew the danger of being caught out upon that mowed flat, so far from any houses, for the nearest dwelling was that of a farmer across Gull Lake, two miles and a half to the southeast.

He had not much time to think or to exercise his fears before the great storm was upon them.

It was nothing less than a hurricane from the beginning, and at the first fierce gust the big unwieldly rack careened with its load so that the little girls screamed with fright, and the horses stopped and stood turning their heads away from the pelting sleet which drove down at the first burst of the storm.

The air was filled instantly with the driving ice.

Dick shouted at the animals and slapped at them with the lines, but they could not be induced to turn their heads against the storm. They stood as if paralyzed by the fierce blast of wind and sleet. Another and more furious sweep of the hurricane came almost immediately, and this time the rack was lifted completely off the sled and overturned with hay and riders.

Fortunately, there was a considerable drift of snow beside the road, and neither Dick nor the younger children were hurt by the fall. They had all, with a common impulse, jumped from the top of the load as it careened over, and so fell, or rather tumbled, outside the sweep of the rack.

As they scrambled to their feet the stiff wind was so filled with hay and snow that they could scarcely distinguish each other. The rack turned bottom side up, and, as it was built in the shape of a "figure four" quail trap, held most of the hay securely beneath its frame.

Dick still held to one of the lines, and the horses stood shivering with fear and cold, for the temperature had suddenly dropped far below the freezing point.

"Get behind the rack out of the wind!" he screamed to the younger ones, who were clinging to each other in the endeavor to stand up before the raging wind. They obeyed him, and, hugging close against the framework, found themselves protected from the cutting blast, but snow and sleet whirled over the top and about the ends in blinding scurries.

Dick knew instinctively that to attempt to get those children on the bare sled and to drive them to a place of safety only meant certain death to them all. In the first place, it would require all their strength to cling on. Moreover, they could not endure a half-hour even of such exposure to the storm. With darkness coming on and the air filled with driving snow, there was the barest possibility of his being able to find a house—it could only be found by running against it or into a yard—even if he should be able to drive and keep the children alive all night.

His plans were quickly made, and a man twice his age could not have made them with greater good sense, or have shown a braver spirit in their execution.

He stripped the harness from his horses and turned them loose. Then, without waiting even to see which direction the animals took, he ran to his brothers and sisters.

Although it had been so warm when they started from home, their mother had insisted that Jeanie and Carrie should dress warmly, and take cloaks and comforters with them. These they had put on before the storm came, and Dick, after digging in the hay for a few minutes between the boards of the rack, discovered the horse-blankets upon which the children had fortunately been sitting when the load overturned.

While digging for them he had prepared a "nest," as he termed it, for the three small ones, and he now ordered them to get in there while he tucked the blankets around them. Frightened and hushed by the terrific storm, they obeyed without a murmur, and the brave young fellow told them that they must "cuddle close together and never peep outside" till they heard him call them.

He said that he would go and bring them something to eat as soon as he could get back from Mr. Waldeman's across Gull Lake, and then after the blizzard was over they would all go home.

He knew the snow would drift over them in a very

few minutes, and believed that if they kept quiet their breath would warm the "nest" and no doubt keep them alive for many hours. But he knew also that such blizzards have been known to last with unabated fury for two or three days, and that there was little likelihood of their being able to outlast such a storm. Therefore, his only hope was to reach help if possible, and get it to them the moment it should be possible to breast the blizzard.

Gull Lake lay over a mile distant, directly to the southeast. It was one mile and a half across it, and on the other side lay Waldeman's ranch, a large group of buildings, dwelling, barns and shedding for stock, enclosed by a large yard which stretched along the lake shore for forty rods or more.

Dick hoped that he might be able to reach this ranch and to find it.

Buttoning his overcoat tightly about him and pulling a "Norwegian cap" which he wore tightly down over his ears, he set out, going directly with the storm, which came from the northwest.

He started at a stiff run. The wind nearly lifted him off his feet at every step, and cut the backs of his legs and the sides of his cheeks icily.

He soon found it impossible to tell whether he was going directly with the wind or not, as it blew in changeful gusts and whirled violently about him. But there was a mile of lake shore in front, and he reached it at length and found himself upon the ice.

It had now grown dark, and amidst the pitchy blackness of night and the thick drift of snow he could no longer make use of his eyes. In fact, he was obliged to shut them and allow himself to be carried

over the ice by the wind. A part of the time he was
able to keep his feet, but often he was thrown forward
and actually blown over the rough ice for rods. The
skirt of his overcoat occasionally blew over his head,
and the bitter wind pierced every part of his body.

It was a rough and terrible experience getting across
the lake, and he was glad he had not attempted to take
his brother and sisters with him.

When he at length reached the southern bank, he
was so chilled and exhausted that he could scarcely
keep his feet at all. The bank was high at the point
where he reached it, and he knew it could not be
opposite the ranch fence, as the high bank was west of
that. So he turned, and alternately walked and
crawled eastward, guided in that direction by the wind.

For a long time he forced his way along the edge of
the ice, which was swept bare, guided by the sense of
feeling and the direction of the wind, but at length he
stumbled against something and joyfully discovered it
to be a fence.

As it afterward proved, it was an extension of the
cattle-yard, a corner of which was built down into the
edge of the lake to afford water for the stock, and had
he missed it by even a few feet he would undoubtedly
have perished.

The discovery of it gave him new life at once and
aroused all his faculties. He climbed over the fence so
as to get inside the yard, and then, by feeling, followed
it until he came to a connection with the cattle-sheds.

Once in the shelter of these, he whipped his numbed
arms and stamped his chilled feet until circulation was
partly restored, then felt his way along to the barn, and
at length managed to reach the ranch dwelling, guided

by the glimmer of a light which he could see through the storm.

He was welcomed and warmed and fed, and promised that by every possible effort that could be made the men should help him to rescue his brother and sisters when daylight came.

Dick found that he had escaped with only a slight frosting of his face and fingers, but his anguish on account of the little ones he had left buried in the hay was intense. He did not sleep at all, but walked the floor of the ranch kitchen, where he was allowed to keep a roaring fire all night. Every few moments he would go to the windows, scratch the frost, and endeavor to peer out into the storm.

He could gather no encouragement until daylight, when he discovered that the snow was no longer falling, and that the sky would soon be clear.

He roused the ranch hands at once, as two of them had agreed to go with him.

In a short time the men were up. Some hot coffee was drunk, a jug of it was filled from the pot, and a sharp-shod team was harnessed. The horses were blindfolded, their heads wrapped in blankets to protect them from the blinding drift which was still driving hard from the northwest.

This team was hitched to a double sleigh filled with robes and wraps. Then, muffling themselves in the bottom of the box, the party set out across the lake in the very teeth of the wind.

The horses were old and steady, and, after some snorting and tossing of the heads, as a protest against the novelty of complete "blinds," took a steady hard trot over the corrugated ice.

On reaching the farther shore of the lake and ascending to the prairie, Dick, with his head completely muffled to the eyes, took a standing position and, bracing himself, directed the movements of the driver. The short distance of a mile and the steady direction of the wind enabled him to hit the hay-road at a point so close to the overturned rack that he caught sight of the top of it as they were passing some rods distant.

A moment later they had halted and tied the team, and Dick had pointed out the spot where his companions were to dig. Then, utterly overcome, he threw himself upon the drift and buried his face in his arms. His grief and suspense at that moment were almost beyond endurance He had no idea that the children could have survived such a fearful night. But five minutes of silent digging occupied his companions, and at the end of that time both of them gave a triumphant shout.

They had uncovered the nest and a cloud of steam rose up from the blankets. Dick was on his feet instantly. A moment later the three young Jordans were dragged forth, alive, but stupid with cold and a drowsiness which would not have left them alive many hours longer. Yet they had escaped any serious frostbite, and a dexterous rubbing, shaking and jouncing restored their circulation and their senses. They were bundled into the sleigh amid robes and comforters, and, despite the severity of the weather and the drifting snow, were taken immediately toward home, where their welcome must be imagined

One of Dick's horses perished in the storm; but the other turned up alive and well the next day at a farmer's stables twelve miles south of Gull Lake.

XII.

A FORTUNATE CYCLONE.

"Ben down to 'Squire Brennan's, Mose?"

The speaker was a sturdy farmer, who stood mopping the moisture from his brow just outside the lane fence which divided his snug farm from that of his nearest neighbor.

Moses Bently drew the reins tightly across the neck of his dripping horse, and with a sharp "Whoa!" flung himself out of the saddle.

"Yes," said he; "I've ben thar;" and pulling a huge bandanna from his pocket, he took off his hat and followed the example of his neighbor across the fence.

"Jones," exclaimed he, with vehemence, "but ain't this a scorcher? Never seed sech hot weather in the last of August. Cuttin' up corn, air ye? Bless me, man! you'll drop fust ye know, an' hev to be laid in the shade."

"Not's long's I can keep up a sweat," replied Jones, coming forward from the corn shocks and leaning upon the fence. "But say, Mose, what's that rumpus 'bout over in your neighborhood? What's the row 'tween Blake an' Miller, anyhow? I hear they've ben down to Brennan's lawin' it to-day."

"Yaas," returned Moses, "they've ben thar lawin' it, an' they're likely to keep on lawin' to the end o' ther days. But mercy, Jones! I can't stand in this hot sun tellin' ye 'bout it."

"Come under the shadder o' this plum-tree here,"

walking toward a large branching plum which stood, loaded with fruit, just inside the fence. "Here's a good place to set down an' cool yerself off," he added, as Mose finished tying his animal and climbed over the fence.

"Yaas," said Moses, again, as he seated himself beside Jones at the foot of the tree, lifted his broad-brimmed straw hat and drew one hickory shirt sleeve across his beady forehead. "Yaas, they'll law it now s' long's they live, an' in the end all they'll have'll go to pay up costs. I left their lawyers argyin' 'fore Squire Brennan, an' a picked jury that didn't know nothin' 'bout the case, nor nothin' 'bout anything else if I'm any judge; jest like most o' the men that gets on juries, though; lot o' loafers, reg'lar nuisances, that's just got pride 'nough t' keep 'em out o' the poorhouse.

"Squire Brennan did his best, jest as he al'ays does, to get 'em to settle; but bless ye! 'twa'n't any use. They're madder 'n hornets, both of 'em. I went down as a witness, but what I knew didn't amount to nothin' 'n' I jest got disgusted with their wranglin', an' when they was done with me I come away an,"—

"But what's it all about?" broke in Jones. "Air they fightin' 'bout that new survey?"

"Waal, yaas, that's at the bottom of it, but they wouldn't had no trouble 'bout that, I guess, if 't hadn't been for them harvest-apple trees on Blake's line, that he set out when he first moved onto the place. There's only five or six of em, and they don't bear a great sight of apples, either; but they're good, what there is of 'em, an' dead ripe now. You see, Blake sot 'em out right on his south line, or jest as near as he could, an' not have 'em grow so's to spread acrost. Wall, the

Gov'ment surveyors was jest as drunk when they run the lines over Section Twelve as they was when they laid out the rest o' this township, an' so this new survey sets them apple-trees jest inside Miller's north line.

"There ain't any question, of course," continued Moses, "not the least sprinklin' o' doubt that Miller's got a legal right to them apple-trees, ef the last survey is c'rect, an' he's mean enough—which it seems he is— to claim 'em. But it seems that Blake hadn't no idea that Miller would lay any claim to the apples, or that he re'ly intended to have the line-fence sot over, bein' as 'twas only a matter of two feet or so, an' 'specially so long's there was a chance to dispute the last lay-out an' set up the old Gov'ment one agin.

"The new survey, ye know, was made last June, an' the change o' lines 'tween Blake an' Miller was so leetle that Blake never thought o' speakin' of it, only jest in a jokin' way. Ye see, the west line o' Section Twelve was changed much as three rods; but as the odds was all in favor of both of 'em, an' had to come out o' the public road, which hadn't ben used but four years, they both felt toler'ble good over it.

"But as I was sayin', Blake hadn't no idea that Miller'd make trouble about the middle line, as there was a good solid fence that they'd both built atween 'em; but when his apples got ripe, he went down one day an' begun pickin' some off'm the earliest tree. An' while he was a-pickin' of 'em, here comes one o' Miller's boys, with a bag slung over his arm, an' climbs over the fence.

"'Mornin', Joe!' says Blake, unsuspectin' as could be. 'Got through harvestin'?'

"'Yes,' says Joe. 'Thought we'd better git some o' these apples, now they're gittin' ripe. Pop says they belong to him now, but you can have half of 'em this year, bein' as you put out the trees; or he'll pay ye for your trouble in settin' 'em out.'

"'He will, hay?' snaps Blake, settin' down his pail an' starin' at young Joe sarcastical like. 'Your dad's a mighty generous fellow, aint he, now? He'll *give* me half the apples! GIVE 'em to me, will he? Waal, I guess he will, for I sh'll take 'em, the whole of 'em, not only this year, but ev'ry year, and don't ye forget that now, sonny!'

"At that, Joe, he kinder bridled up a leetle. 'I guess my father's got a right in the lan',' says he. 'An' he told me to pick some o' these apples, an' I'm goin' to take some of 'em home now,' and eyin' Blake kind o' cautious-like, he reached up for a big yaller one that hung a-tempting his jaws just above his head.

"'Don't you touch that!' yells Blake, starting for him in a way that made the boy dodge from under the tree an' scramble for dear life over the fence.

"Waal, of course Miller was madder 'n a hornet, an' so, with his new survey back of him, he goes down to Squire Brennan's and sues Blake for trespass, an' sence that time each one of 'em's had one o' *their* boys watchin' them apples, day an' night, to see 't other'n didn't steal 'em. They mount guard out there like a couple o' roosters, one on one side the fence an' the other on t'other. One of 'em's afraid to touch the apples, an' the other dasn't."

"What'll be the outcome, think?" asked Jones, as Moses paused in his narrative, and again made use of the huge bandanna.

"The outcome? Bless you, man, there won't be no outcome to it. Squire Brennan can't decide the case, an' if he did, 'twouldn't amount to nothin', an' no decidin' ever will so long's there's a higher court to carry the thing through, an' then they'll take a fresh start an' go through agin. This is a case, ye see, for trespass, but how're they goin' to make trespass out of it till they can prove who the land belongs to?"

"I see," said Jones; "goin' to be a nice wrangle, ain't it?"

"I s'h'd say so," muttered Moses. "But, Jones," he added, getting upon his feet, "I must be goin'. Do you see that black cloud off in the southwest? Shouldn't wonder if we'd git another reg'lar old twister when that comes up, an it's a-comin', too."

"Thought I heard it thunderin' an' kind o' rumblin somewhar a bit ago," said Jones, rising. "I'm 'fraid you're right, Mose, and I don't know but it *is* a good plan for a feller to be gettin' around close't to his suller."

"Yaas," returned Moses. "My wife and the young ones have jest about half-lived in my dug-out this summer. Every time they see a cloud, they skedaddle for 'the house of refuge,' as Sarah calls it."

"Beats all how many o' them tornadoes goes ragin' over this country lately," said Jones; "'pears like a man aint safe nowheres," and bidding each other good-day, the two men separated.

"TWISTER," as a word in Western parlance, has attained an entirely new signification within the last two years, especially throughout the now famous storm belt extending from central Kansas in a northwesterly direction beyond the southern boundary of Minnesota.

The prevalence of those terrible storms known as tornadoes, cyclones, and throughout this region as "twisters," has become so alarming of late that in some of the counties of Iowa the citizens take refuge in their cellars during the summer season at the appearance of every dark and threatening cloud.

In this region a large proportion of the farmers and many of the townspeople dig out-of-door cellars, or "under-ground houses," in which to shelter themselves from the violence of these atmospheric disturbances.

On nearing one of their dwellings, one notices, but a few yards to one side, a heaped-up mound of earth, with an opening in one end disclosing the frame-work and top of a heavy door, the bottom of which is reached by a flight of steps cut into the earth in front. The whole is constructed much after the pattern of the summer milk-house of more Eastern farmers, and indeed, most of the dug-outs are used for that purpose also.

The genuine tornado, or "twister,"—the one which tears up everything in its track,—is generally preceded by a short time of hot, "muggy" weather, and at such times, when the feather-edged, dark-centred nimbus floats lazily a mile or two above the farmer's head, small spiral-shaped projections are often seen suddenly darting downward from their centres, curling, twisting, steadily shooting ahead, sometimes almost reaching the earth. Then, with a peculiar, writhing motion, these snake-like columns of vapor break up into little sections, or separate puffs, and disappear as quickly as they were formed.

Sometimes a dozen or more may be seen at a single glance. On such days it is necessary to be on the lookout, and if the cloud above one of those dark columns grows suddenly black and emits flashes of lightning, followed by the rumble of thunder, the "dug-out" is the only safe retreat.

About three o'clock on the particular afternoon and near the locality of which we write, the thermometer at various places indicated 98° Fahrenheit in the shade, and away towards the horizon in the south and west could be seen piled-up masses of silver-tinted thunder-clouds, their lowering bases sinking almost out of sight behind the distant woods and fields.

"My! what whoppin' old thunder-heads!" thought Billings Blake, as he sat sweltering beneath the shade of one of the disputed apple-trees; "guess Clem Miller'll get sick of his bargain sittin' over there on the south side of the fence. He dasn't come over here, though," he soliloquized, "'cause he knows I c'n lick 'im the best day he ever saw, an' he knows I will, too, if he comes."

Clem did have a pretty hard place, to be sure; for, to tell the truth, he was afraid of young Blake, and so, as there were no trees on his side, he was obliged to content himself with the small shelter afforded by the green corn-stalks which grew beside the fence.

"I wish pa'd never made any row 'bout these miserable old apple-trees," he grumbled, as he held his broad-brimmed hat high over his head in order to shelter himself from the scorching rays which would find their way down through the corn leaves; "I don't want to be melted into taller a-watching them old apples that'll rot in two days after they're picked. I don't like the looks of them clouds," he added, a moment later.

"Haloo, Clem!"

Could he believe his ears? Yes, it was surely young Billings Blake calling him.

"Want's me to come over there, and then lick me," growled Clem.

"I say, Clem," bawled young Blake again. "Clem, jest get up an' look over the hill yender. I believe there's a twister a-comin'."

Clem got up and looked.

"'Tis sure enough, Bill," he answered. "Do ye reckon it will come this way sure?"

"Dun no," said Billings. "I say, Clem, come over here an' let's watch the thing!"

It is curious how a common danger transforms the bitterest enemies into the best of friends. Clem got over the fence without the slightest hesitation, and in a moment the two boys, who just before would not have deigned to speak to each other, stood together, gazing in common fear and wonder upon a scene that once witnessed is never forgotten.

Away to the southwest, several of those silvery-edged, harmless-looking clouds had grown together, and were rapidly approaching. Their sun-tinted columns had suddenly changed color, and, black and angry, they were tumbling together in ugly broken masses, while forks of jagged lightning darted across their lowering sides, and the distant growl of thunder could be distinctly heard.

The wind sprang up, and began to stir the leaves of the apple-trees, and to rustle the broad blades of corn, while black masses of vapor swept hurriedly across the sky, obscuring the sun, and hurling themselves into the very midst of the huge pile, thus constantly swelling its already enormous proportions.

"Mercy!" said Clem, catching at his hat as a fresh gust of wind swept past. "Mercy! Bill, the wind's a-blowin' from ev'ry direction, an' jest look at them clouds; they're a-comin' from every way, an' goin' every where. Don't ye think we'd better git for shelter?"

"Where sh'll we go, Clem, to better ourselves?" asked his companion. "Ye can't tell where she'll strike the hardest, and fer one, I'd rather be in the open field than in the woods when there's a hurricane comin'. But jest look at 'er."

Even as he spoke, the roar of the approaching hurricane drowned his voice, and a round black column, darting down from the center of the hurrying mass, struck the timber across the hill with a roar and a crash that was fairly deafening.

"Run, Clem! Git for the field!" yelled Bill; and the frightened boys scurried away toward the north, and the fifty yards' run which they were then able to make probably saved their lives.

On came the twisting, writhing storm, tearing the earth, trees, grain and fences in its track, and filling the air with a hideous din. Swiftly as the boys ran, they were not fleet-footed enough to escape the effect of the fearful side wind which accompanied the whirling cloud.

Clem felt his legs suddenly wrenched from under him, and in a trice found himself turning the most astonishing summersaults he had ever dreamed of. His hat and shirt were literally torn away from him, and a moment later, scratched, bruised, and lacerated by the corn stubs over which he had been tumbled, he found himself lying on his back in a deep, dead furrow, with six inches of muddy water slushing around him.

Bill had fared but little better, as, spattered with mud and bleeding from half-a-dozen bruises, he picked himself up from between two corn rows, where he had been carried bodily.

"We are in a bad fix, sure," said Bill. "But jest look down yonder in the track of 'er, will ye? There's a strip forty rods wide where there aint a thing standin', an' the ground's all ploughed ready for winter wheat. Yes, an'—an'—an'—can I believe my eyes—*the apple trees are gone!*"

"If they haint!" answered Clem. "Hurrah, Bill! your dad an' mine'll quit their quarrellin' now, won't they, an' we'll all be friends an hunt ducks together like we used to?"

www.ingramcontent.com/pod-product-compliance
Lightning Source LLC
Chambersburg PA
CBHW022134160426
43197CB00009B/1274